The Angler's Library

BOAT FISHING

The Angler's Library

BOAT FISHING

by
TREVOR HOUSBY

Illustrations by
GRAHAM ALLEN

BARRIE & JENKINS
COMMUNICA-EUROPA

First published 1971 by
Barrie & Jenkins Ltd
2 Clement's Inn London WC2
Revised impression, 1978

ISBN 0 214 65298 x

Printed in Great Britain by
Redwood Burn Limited
Trowbridge & Esher

dedicated
to Ilda

Contents

Introduction

DURING the past decade, sea fishing has become extremely popular in most areas of the British Isles. Even in remote places local charter-fishing industries are springing up to cater for the needs and requirements of an ever-increasing number of sea fishermen who are more than willing to travel long distances to catch the fish they want. This new breed of sea anglers has revolutionised sea fishing to such an extent that tackle firms are continually working on new items of tackle and improvements to existing gear. This is necessary, for there is an increasing demand for up-to-date rods, reels, lines, etc., that can be used with the new techniques which are now being devised and developed. The boat-angling image has changed radically during the past ten years. 'Broom-handle' wood or cane rods are now out in favour of lightweight fibre-glass models with a lifting strength which belies their frail outward appearance. Reels, too, are changing and nowadays it is rare to see a boat angler fishing with a wooden (or even metal) centre-pin reel. This is the multiplier age, and English, American and European companies are producing a wide range of such reels specifically for the boat angler. There is no doubt that modern tackle has revolution-ised boat fishing, for the lightweight rods and reels and fine nylon or braided Terylene lines can be used to overcome many of the problems which confronted the old-time boat angler. Even in areas where the tides are too fierce to use conventional lines, the new range of steel lines that have become available can be used to take the bait down to the bottom where the fish congregate and feed. Only recently I used a stainless steel line while turbot fishing on the famous Shambles Bank, off Weymouth, Dorset. On this occasion the usual heavy tides were roaring over the lip of the Bank, causing the Weymouth anglers to use 5- and 6-lb. lead 'bombs' to hold bottom. I was the only one in the boat using a wire line and the advantage of this type of line material was obvious, for where the others used their massive leads I was able to fish comfortably with weights ranging from 10 to 16 oz. At slack water I reduced this to less than 2 oz. and was still able to hold bottom in an area that normally calls for at least 2 lb. of lead even at the slowest stage of the tidal run. Stainless steel lines are still very much of a new thing, but from using them for over a year without losing a single fish through breakage, I can confidently say that single-strand wire has a tremendous future in boat fishing and when boat anglers in general come to accept its potential for fishing in difficult tidal areas, it will become a standard part of most boat anglers' equipment. Wreck fishermen have already used it to take massive catches of near-record conger, ling and cod, and I am quite convinced that the wire will bring about a whole new series of techniques during the next few seasons, techniques that may bring about the downfall of a number of record-breaking specimens.

Quite apart from a general improvement in tackle, the new boom in sea angling has created an industry which calls for a high-quality boat built and maintained specifically for charter-fishing expeditions. Good boats skippered by competent and knowledgeable men are now available in most of the popular fishing ports and with competition becoming fiercer each successive season, charter-boat owners are endeavouring to move with the times by changing their craft at regular intervals for larger, faster boats of improved design. At the same time the skippers of these boats also try to improve their own knowledge of the grounds they fish and the angling techniques required so that they can find fish for their charter parties even on days when the more productive offshore marks are out of reach due to rough weather. Along my own section of the Hampshire coast I find the standards of the local boatmen and their craft to be extremely high, and at Lymington the boatmen run regular exploratory trips to try to locate specific fish or new fishing grounds for the anglers they take out. I also travel considerable distances to fish from other venues and find that most of the boatmen I meet do their absolute utmost to ensure a good day for each party they take out. High-grade electronic instruments now help to locate specific marks and very few boats now sail without having an echo sounder aboard as standard equipment. Some of the bigger boats specialising in wreck fishing also use the complicated and comparatively expensive Decca navigator sets which are so essential for locating wrecks in deep-water areas well offshore. At present this accurate navigational aid is used by a few boats, but by the mid 1970s many charter boats will

10

carry equipment of this kind. Many boatmen of course still use the old system of cross bearings to pinpoint the marks they fish, but as a general rule this technique is being rapidly replaced by modern electronic equipment. Basically, boat fishing on modern lines is still in its infancy, but I feel that it is now entering its most interesting stage of development. A similar situation was experienced by freshwater anglers during the early 1950s when a handful of expert anglers set out to prove that by revising tackle and techniques it would be quite possible to catch large fish in undreamed of quantities. As a direct result of this initial effort several national records were smashed and a whole new field of angling was opened. The tactics and techniques devised by the original anglers have since been enlarged upon and improved by specimen hunters all over the country, with the result that big fish captures are now a fairly commonplace occurrence for the average angler who is willing to adopt an intelligent approach to his fishing. A similar upsurge of new ideas and tackle is now beginning to show up in boat-fishing circles, and today's modern angler is going to sea to catch specific types of fish. A typical example being conger, a species which has attracted a lot of interest in recent seasons. The old conger record has of course been broken twice already as a direct result of specialised fishing, and will no doubt go again now that anglers realise that by adopting specialised techniques it is quite possible to catch fish approaching record size at fairly frequent intervals. I can foresee that in the future, specimen hunting at sea will become as rewarding as specimen hunting in freshwater, and this will no doubt lead to a lot of highly interesting discoveries being made. Boat angling, then, is well on its way up, but the best is yet to come and, like so many keen sea fishermen, I am glad to be in on the ground floor of a sport which holds so much promise for future seasons.

CHAPTER I

Skate, Ray, Monk and Angler Fish

FOR many years, all skates and rays have been classed under the general heading of either thornback ray or common skate. In other words, every small specimen has been automatically regarded as a thornback ray and every big one as a common skate irrespective of its species. The record lists and the sea-angling clubs have equally been responsible for this sorry state of affairs, and it is only during the past five years that anglers have become aware of the various species. But even now it is common to see spotted, small-eyed or sandy ray being weighed in as thornbacks, and I shudder to think how many potential record-breakers have been brought to the scales and classified as medium-sized thornbacks in club record books.

Fortunately, anglers are becoming increasingly record conscious and many individuals are now taking the trouble to learn to identify the various types of skate and ray. Club fishermen, on the other hand, still adopt a couldn't-care-less attitude, and most are just content to bring fish to the scales to boost their end-of-season weight. To a large extent, club officials are the ones to blame for this lack of interest and knowledge—bearing in mind, of course, that the organisation of a club competition and subsequent end-of-day weigh-in leaves little spare time for sorting out and identifying various fish which are basically very similar in outward appearance. No doubt, however, the day will come when each weigh-in will include a steward whose sole job will be to identify individual species as they are brought to the scales.

To help clarify this situation, there follows a fairly detailed account of the various types of skate and ray found around our shores. Knowing just what fish you have caught adds to the overall pleasure of angling; and one day it may be a record-breaker. Many of the records on the British list are open, and others are held by fish with very low weights which should be easy to equal or beat if luck is on your side. It must be every angler's dream to catch a record-breaker. I know it is one of my own angling ambitions. On several occasions I

13

have been within a few ounces of achieving my goal—but a miss is as good as a mile, although I still live in hope.

Thornback Ray

The thornback is one of the commonest of British rays, and in many areas it is one of the most sought-after fish. As its name implies, it has a number of thorny spines on its back and tail. These can be very sharp, and it is wise to handle a freshly caught thornback ray very carefully to avoid injury. Most anglers carry an old piece of towelling with which to pick up these spiky fish.

The thornback is variable in coloration, usually brown or greyish brown on the back. This basic colour is overlaid with pale spots surrounded by borders of small dark spots. Small-ish fish have banded tails, but the bands are often absent on large specimens. The underparts are white.

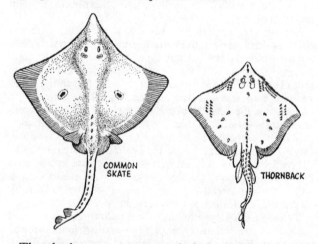

COMMON SKATE

THORNBACK

Thornback grow to a comparatively large size, and specimens to nearly 40 lb. have been taken. The average run of rod-caught fish weigh between 7 and 12 lb.—a twenty-pounder being regarded as a good catch in most areas.

These fish have a wide distribution and can be found in most places round the British Isles. They are plentiful in the English Channel, and some of the sea lochs in the Western

Highlands of Scotland are thick with them. They are commonest where the sea bed is comprised of sand, mud or gravel, but they can sometimes be caught over rocks as well. The skate grounds off the Isle of Wight are often a mixture of rock and flat clay mud, and these areas seem to produce larger than average thornback during most months of the year.

Thornback ray are generally regarded as a summer species, but I have found that it is possible to catch good bags of these fish during the winter months. During the spring and summer months, they often feed in comparatively shallow water. In the winter, they tend to move offshore on to the deeper marks. Thornbacks, like all the skates and rays, are bottom feeders which live by eating any crustaceans, worms and small fish they can catch or find dead. And again like the other members of their tribe, thornbacks tend to be scavengers and will eat any stale baits the angler cares to use. Along the Hants coast many of the successful thornback specialists swear by a stinking bait and make a point of leaving their herring or mackerel baits in the sun until they consider that they are 'smelly' enough to attract hunting thornbacks.

Catches would show that thornback ray usually travel in small groups, each group consisting of one female followed by several male fish. The female is usually the largest fish in the group and seems to be given first refusal of any food the group happens to come across, for more often than not it is the female that is caught first. Once the female has been caught, the male fish seem to hang about under the boat and are often caught in quick succession. Very occasionally, an exceptionally large group of ray might be encountered. The last time I found such a group, my companion and I had 22 ray between our two rods. This was an unusually large catch of fish which I doubt very much I will ever repeat.

Blonde Ray

During the past two seasons, several very large blonde ray have been caught by south-coast anglers—as a result of which a new record for the species has been established. Unfortunately, a real record-breaker of nearly 40 lb. was eaten before its captor realised just what a monster he had boated. This fish was taken from Brian Macnamara's charter boat *Bonito II* from a well-known ray mark off Freshwater Bay, Isle of Wight. A similar record-breaker was caught off Swanage, Dorset, during the 1969 season. This, again, was cut up and distributed before any official had the opportunity to examine the body.

In shape, the blonde ray is less angular than the thornback and it lacks the large thornlike spines. It is usually sandy-coloured on the back, with a thick sprinkling of small black spots which extend to the margins of its wings. There are also nine or ten round pale patches on the body disc. The underparts are white.

Blonde ray grow, on average, to a larger size than the thornback but are seldom caught in any quantity. They are common in the Channel and on the Atlantic coast, but seem to be rather rare in the North Sea. Most of the blonde ray I have caught or examined have been taken in fairly deep water.

Hermit crab seems to be a favourite food of the blonde ray, although most of the fish caught by rod-and-line anglers fall to fish fillet baits of various types.

Homelyn or Spotted Ray

The spotted ray is often confused with the blonde ray, for at first glance both fish have a similar basic appearance. However, the nose or snout of the spotted ray is rather more prominent than that of the true blonde ray and the overall colouring of the back is darker. The pale spots, although present on the back of the spotted ray, are less well defined than those on the blonde ray—although on the few specimens I have seen there has always been a single prominent pale blotch on each wing. In every case, this has been bordered by a ring of small dark spots.

Spotted ray are found all around our coasts, generally in fairly shallow water. Although smaller than the blonde ray, they can be caught on large baits. Most of those I have caught, or heard of, have nevertheless been taken on worm baits intended for plaice.

Cuckoo Ray

This fish is easy to identify. Its heart-shaped body and yellowish-brown back is most distinctive. To make identifica-

16

tion even simpler there is a large dark eye-spot on each wing, superimposed on which are yellow spots and wavy lines.

Cuckoo ray have a wide distribution and, although by no means commonly caught, they have been recorded from most

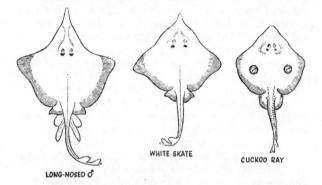

LONG-NOSED ♂

WHITE SKATE

CUCKOO RAY

parts of our coasts. Like the spotted ray, most of the specimens taken have fallen to worm baits. Cuckoo ray are probably the smallest ray, most of the fish I have examined having weighed between 1½ and 3 lb.

Painted Ray

The painted ray is also easy to identify, for its sandy-coloured back is covered with a series of dark lines and artistic blotches. The angling Press has nicknamed this fish the 'pop-art ray'—a name which suits it admirably, with its back resembling the work of a modernistic artist.

Painted ray seem to be common in the eastern half of the Channel, and odd specimens have also been caught off South Devon. Most specimens taken weigh between 8 and 14 lb. Like the thornback, the painted ray is a scavenger and can be caught on fish baits.

Small-eyed Ray

During the 1969 season, there was a sudden influx of small-eyed ray into marks along the south coast. A number of fish of record-breaking size were taken, and some large bags of average specimens were recorded. At first, many of the fish were mistaken for medium-sized blonde ray, which they closely resemble. Prior to this invasion, the only area from which I had ever caught small-eyed ray was a small patch of mixed clay and rock off Freshwater Bay. Then, suddenly, the fish were everywhere—from the Straits of Dover down to Land's End. The Channel was alive with them. Whether or not they will continue to come in future years it is impossible to say, but I hope so. They provide good sport on light tackle and make excellent eating.

In shape, the small-eyed ray is similar to the blonde ray; but in colour, it is a much paler fish. All the specimens I have seen have been a sandy colour on the back, with a series of pale spots and lines—the lines being most apparent on the outer extremities of the wings. The edges of the wings and also the tail are outlined in brilliant white, giving the fish an overall neatness and clean-cut appearance.

Small-eyed ray are bold biters, and they often hook themselves as they pick up the bait and move away with it.

Sting Ray

The sting ray is a rather localised species which the vast majority of sea anglers may never have the opportunity to catch. The only places known to me where sting ray are at all common are the Solent and the Essex coast. Individual specimens have, however, been taken from many places in the Channel, and can crop up at almost any point around the British Isles.

On average, sting ray attain a large size, a twenty-pounder being generally regarded as a small specimen. My best sting ray tipped the scales at 35 lb., but fish up to almost twice this weight have been caught. A Clacton angler, for example, caught a monster sting ray in 1952. This fish, although never weighed properly, was estimated to weigh around 70 lb. In the Lymington area of the Solent, sting ray of around 40 lb. are caught during the course of most seasons; and a trawlerman working the Solent in 1966 caught and released a monster ray thought to weigh 100 lb. This huge fish was minus its whiplike tail—a sure sign that at some time in its life it had been caught by an angler, for in many areas beach anglers who catch a sting ray make a habit of chopping off the fish's tail before attempting to remove the hook.

Sting ray are very similar in shape to skate, but they have a rounder overall outline. In colour, they are normally drab brown with no spots or blotches, the underparts being a mottled white-grey. The body of the fish is covered in a disgusting layer of thick, evil-smelling slime.

TORPEDO RAY   STING RAY

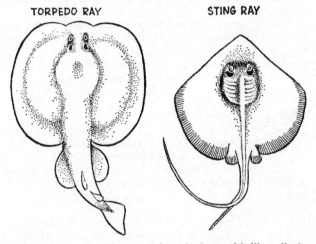

The sting-ray gets its name from its long whiplike tail, the jagged, bony spine of which can cause a very nasty wound. The fish has an unpleasant habit of swishing this formidable weapon about, and it is to avoid accidents that most anglers chop the tail off the moment the fish is boated or landed. The tail spine is grooved and carries venom which can cause an intensely painful wound and temporary paralysis. Several anglers I know have been cut by the thrashing tail of a big ray and each has suffered very badly as a result.

Sting ray are a summer species and the best months to try for them are June and July, when they are normally to be found in shallow water. Very little is known about their movements in English waters. The general belief is that they migrate offshore during the winter months. I am inclined to believe, however, that they spend the winter months in hibernation in the thick mud of the Solent or the Essex creeks and marshes.

Although I have known of sting ray taking fish baits, their

19

favourite food is, without doubt, lug or ragworm. The boat angler who wants to catch these fish in any quantity will be well advised to employ these worms as bait. Sting ray also feed to a lesser extent on crabs and shellfish, and I have hooked several on hermit crab baits. Some people do eat sting ray; but unless I am particularly asked for one, I make a habit of returning all those I catch to the sea. They are messy fish to handle, and there is little point in killing them just to show them off to friends.

Sting ray often travel in large groups, and where you catch one you can usually be sure to get a few more. In spite of their ungainly shape and repulsive appearance, they can provide good sport on reasonably light tackle, for they are powerful creatures capable of short bursts of terrific speed.

Electric or Torpedo Ray

This is not a fish which the average boat angler is likely to catch or even see; but the odd specimen has been taken on rod and line, and for this reason I feel it is essential to include it. Like the sting ray, it can be an ugly customer to handle— and it is better to know what a particular fish is capable of doing before you actually try to touch it.

I have had personal experience of these fish. During the past ten years, I have caught two—the first in a trawl net and the second on rod and line. One weighed over 50 lb., the other just under 40.

Torpedo ray are easy to identify. They have a distinctive shape—the body disc being sub-circular and cut off square across the front, the tail section being similar to, although stouter than, the tail of a monkfish. This fish has two dorsal fins set close to each other near to the wrist of the tail, which rather resembles a broad paddle and tends to sag to one side. The eyes and respiratory holes of the fish are very small, and the skin is devoid of scales and very clammy to the touch. The backs of the fish I caught were slate grey, with no extra markings.

Torpedo ray are known to reach a length of over 5 ft. and a weight of well over 100 lb. An angler fishing off the Quay at Mudeford, in Hampshire, hooked one of over 60 lb. which he eventually landed. The specimen I took on rod and line did not put up much of a fight and was easily brought to the boat.

Torpedo ray live for the most part over soft bottoms, where they feed on fish of all types. Both of those I caught regurgitated quantities of small partially digested sole, from which I can only conclude that torpedo ray feed for the most part on flatfish of one sort or another.

The torpedo fish is a lazy, torpid fish which catches its food by employing an electrical discharge from the powerful 'batteries' in each of its pectoral fins. These batteries are honeycomb-like structures of prism-shaped cells filled with a sort of jelly. The ventral side of the fish is the negative electrode, and the upper side acts as the positive electrode. The sea water completes the circuit through which the substantial current passes. Any small fish which happens to pass close to or touches the ray occasions a reflex action which triggers off an immediate electrical discharge. A fish caught in the path of this discharge is immediately killed or stunned and falls easy prey to the ray. I have heard it said that anyone touching both the upper and the lower surface of a torpedo ray's body at the same time will get a shock comparable with that received from accidentally touching the sparking plug of a car when the engine is running. Even by touching only one side of a ray which is lying on a wet deck may mean getting a slight shock, although this will not occur if you are wearing rubber boots. Because of the danger of this electrical discharge, every sea angler should learn to recognise a torpedo ray at sight. In the event of a catch, and to avoid a shock, the hook should be cut and a new hook tied on in place of the one left in the mouth of the fish. But do not throw the catch overboard: the record for this species is now open to claims.

Three species of skate can be caught in British waters: the common skate; the long-nosed skate; and the white skate, which is sometimes called the bottle-nosed ray. Unlike the ray so far described, all three skate grow to an enormous size and, with the exception of the shark family or the halibut, they are the largest fish the boat angler can expect to encounter around the British Isles.

Common Skate

This fish—occasionally referred to as the grey or blue skate —is, as its major name implies, the commonest of the three large skate and the one most frequently caught by anglers.

In colour, it is greyish brown on the back, with the light-coloured blotches and small dark spots. The underside is grey with dark streaks. Common skate well over 200 lb. have been caught on rod and line. The largest recorded commercially caught specimen weighed 400 lb. and had a measured length of a little over 7 ft.

Common skate are found all round the coasts of Britain, but Scottish and Irish waters produce the most. Fenit in Southern Ireland is a famous common skate port, and at Ullapool in Western Ross an annual skate-fishing championship takes place. Recently, Scapa Flow in the Orkneys has produced a number of very big skate. If all goes well, it would seem likely that the common skate record will change hands regularly from now on, for many of the known big skate grounds are being fished for the first time ever.

I have caught common skate over sand and gravel bottoms, but my best fish have always been hooked on rough mixed ground. A big skate will eat practically any edible object it comes across. An examination of the stomach contents of the large ones I have caught has produced the remains of crabs, lobsters, dogfish, pouting, mackerel and even small skate—proof indeed that a big skate has a large and varied diet sheet.

Long-nosed Skate

This fish is easily recognisable by its abnormally long snout. In colour, it is rather similar to the common skate; but it is a smaller fish, rarely exceeding a length of 5 ft. It has a wide distribution and can be found over similar ground to the common skate. The few specimens that I have hooked have always put up a livelier resistance than common skate of similar size.

White Skate or Bottle-nosed Ray

I was once instrumental in gaffing a record-breaking white skate for a friend of mine. It was a lovely fish, weighing exactly 110 lb., that was caught as a direct result of going out deliberately to fish for large skate on the grounds off the Isle of Wight—the intention being to arrive on the mark just before dark and fish the tide up and down again during the night.

On this occasion, we were blessed with a patch of warm windless weather which gave us the opportunity to stay out overnight, the waters round the Needles area being dangerous in any kind of bad weather. The mark chosen was one which had produced fish of 98 and 100 lb. during the previous season.

To be successful with large skate in this section of the Channel, it is essential to fish during the six-week period starting at the penultimate week in August and finishing at the end of September. Bad weather had already caused us to miss the opening two weeks of this short period. On this our first serious big skate expedition of the year we had high hopes of success. As it happened, we had two reporters from a local and a national paper with us so we felt we had to produce something to save face.

Within ten minutes of anchoring, my companion's rod tip nodded gently two or three times and then slowly pulled hard over as the fish moved off. In typical big skate fashion, it came up against the tide and we knew immediately we had a big fish on. Exactly four hours later the fish made its eleventh long run, convincing us finally that we had a real monster well and truly hooked. Fifty-five minutes after that, in the pre-dawn gloom, the skipper and I got two huge gaffs into the fish and heaved it over the side of the *Bonito I*.

To be honest, we were all disappointed. Although the fish was very big, it was not anywhere near as large as we had thought it would be from its fight. But when we came to take the hook out, we found why it had fought so hard and long and had kept making lengthy and totally unstoppable runs. The hook, instead of being inside the mouth, was caught under the tail of the fish. So although it was a British record for its species, the fish was disqualified simply by being foul-hooked—a bitter disappointment to all concerned but particularly to the man who had caught it. He, incidentally, spent the next week with his arm in a sling, the muscles being cramped and torn from the long hours spent hanging on to a well-bent rod and a fish that fought like a steam train.

So ends the story of a record-breaking white skate: but there will be other occasions no doubt in future seasons when we will once again make positive contact with one of these monster fish that appear off the Isle of Wight during the late summer and early autumn.

The back of the white skate, whose secondary name

derives from the distinctive shape of its snout, is bluish-grey in colour, with paler spots which are very indistinct on the larger fish. The underparts are very white.

White skate are known to reach a length of over 8 ft. and a weight of at least 500 lb. A fish of such size would be a formidable creature to hook on rod and line. Generally, white skate can be regarded as a southern species, small specimens being very common off the coasts of Devon and Cornwall. Their feeding habits are similar to the other large skate, and they also inhabit similar ground.

TACKLE

For the smaller species of ray, a medium-weight hollow- or solid-glass boat rod should be used. Choice of reel is dependent on personal preference, but most anglers find a multiplier suits their requirements best. Although ray are not truly fighting fish, their broad flat bodies and their habit of spiralling up against the pressure of the tide make it impossible to catch them on really light lines. Because of this, most ray fishermen use a 30-lb. b.s. line. All skates and rays have rough strong lips, and although it is possible to catch them on a nylon trace it is more advisable to use a wire link between reel line and hook. I have never actually known a ray to bite through a trace, but I have lost several fish on nylon traces which snapped during the fight. On each occasion, a careful examination of the point of breakage showed that the nylon had been crushed and flattened between the ray's lips. This had immediately become a weak spot and had snapped under the constant pressure.

I lost one huge thornback in this way while fishing off the north coast of Cornwall. The fish, which was hooked in about 100 ft. of water, came up to the surface very quickly, giving everyone on the boat the opportunity to see it clearly and assess its approximate weight. At the time, a strong tide was running. The fish turned broadside on to the flow of water and, within seconds, the line—which should have easily held the weight—parted and the ray sank out of sight. Examination of the trace showed the nylon to be distorted and stretched. Since the loss of this fish, I have never again used a nylon trace for ray. The general opinion was that the fish I had lost weighed at least 30 lb. The thornback of a lifetime gone— simply through using a trace material which weakens when

24

crushed. Even for sting ray I use a nylon-covered wire trace, although the crushing power of the sting ray's lips appears to be less than that of other species.

Choice of hook size for ray fishing depends entirely on the fish you expect to catch and the bait you wish to use. Sting ray, for example, feed best on worm baits, so a smallish hook is essential, my own choice being a size 2-0 stainless-steel Model Perfect—a hook which is small enough to take a worm bait but strong enough to withstand the strain of pumping up to the boat a fish which may well weigh 40 lb. plus. The Model Perfect is, in fact, the only hook of this size that I can recommend for its strength, other makes of similar size having let me down by snapping at the bend or straightening out under pressure. Hooks of this size should also be used for spotted and cuckoo ray.

Thornback, blonde, small-eyed ray, etc., prefer larger baits than the species already mentioned. Because of this, a larger hook must be used, a size 6-0 Model Perfect being ideal for use with fish fillet- or squid-type baits. Model Perfects are

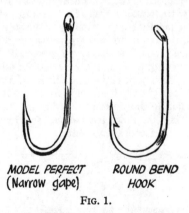

MODEL PERFECT   ROUND BEND
(Narrow gape)   HOOK

FIG. 1.

narrower across the gape (see Fig. 1) than most flat forged hooks of similar size. This, in my opinion, is a useful feature when ray are the quarry—for although most ray have largish mouths, the shape of the mouth is wide rather than deep. I therefore believe that a bait mounted on a hook with a narrow gape is more likely to be taken right away than one that is fastened to a wide gape hook.

BIG SKATE TACKLE

Many a huge skate has been hooked and successfully boated on medium-weight tackle of the type already described; but for every big one caught, a dozen break free and escape during the first few minutes of the fight. Make no mistake: big skate fishing is a rough, tough occupation which calls for rugged tackle and a lot of skill. For years, angling writers have described the fight of a big skate as 'like playing a table-top on a sack of ballast'. From this, I can only assume that these people have never hooked a really large specimen; for although the skate seldom puts up a spectacular fight, its sheer bulk and brute strength make it a dour and formidable opponent.

Most big skate have a habit of clinging to the sea bed, using their huge bodies as a suction disc. These initial tactics make mincemeat out of normal boat tackle. Unless you happen to be fortunate enough to hook a big skate which keeps on the move, a medium boat-fishing outfit will not have the power to lift the fish up from the sea bed without something breaking under the tremendous strain. So I strongly advise anglers who intend to fish for big skate to buy an outfit strong enough to withstand the rigours of this type of angling. A hollow or solid fibre-glass rod of the shark type is essential. This should have a test curve of between 20 and 30 lb. In other words, it will reach its maximum curve when lifting a dead weight of 20 or 30 lb. (see Fig. 2). Rods with either a full set of roller rings or a roller tip ring and fully lined guard rings should be used. Good rings cut down friction and, in a long hard fight, can save the angler considerable effort.

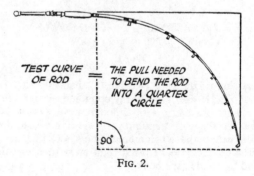

TEST CURVE OF ROD = THE PULL NEEDED TO BEND THE ROD INTO A QUARTER CIRCLE

90°

FIG. 2.

Only two types of reel are of any use for heavy skate fishing: a large capacity multiplier or a centre-pin. My own choice is the Grice and Young Tatler V, but a Penn or Ocean City of similar capacity would be just as good.

The most popular centre-pin type of reel for skate fishing is the Allcocks 'Commodore', which features a special breaking device activated by a projecting lever (see Fig. 3). In my opinion, this reel has two distinct disadvantages. First, it is

ALLCOCKS 'COMMODORE'

FIG. 3.

very heavy. Secondly, when a fish runs and takes line the reel handle revolves at the same speed as the drum and, unless great care is taken, the rapidly spinning handle can easily skin or break the fingers on the reel hand. I had an accident of this type many years ago, while using a large diameter centre-pin for conger fishing. In this instance, the reel handle caught and snapped my second finger, leaving me in acute pain and still attached to an irate conger. The brake lever on the 'Commodore' reel can be brought into play the moment a hooked skate makes off; but even so, accidents can occur. I much prefer to use the multiplier-type reel.

The main reason for using a large capacity reel is so that it can be loaded with at least 300 yards of heavy line—not that big skate normally take out a great length of line on a run, but it's advisable to always have plenty in reserve should the fish decide to run farther than usual. Braided Terylene or Dacron of 50- to 60-lb. should be used, bearing in mind that big skate of over 150 lb. are fairly commonly caught in English, Irish and Scottish waters.

27

Large skate, like most big fish, tend to be rather lazy creatures, preferring one good meal to a lot of snacks. Because of this, it pays to use a generous amount of bait on a large hook: a whole large mackerel or similar-sized fish mounted on a size 8 or 10-0 hook, fastened by crimps to a 4-ft. nylon-covered wire trace which should have a minimum b.s. of 60 lb. This may sound unnecessarily strong; but one should bear in mind that when a big skate is hooked, the trace will be in constant contact with its spiky rough skin and bony lips and will be subjected to considerable wear and tear before the fish is ready for the gaff. I once caught a very big skate while fishing from an ordinary rowing boat on a large Scottish sea loch. This fish, which weighed 145 lb. took over an hour to land, at the end of which time the nylon covering over the actual trace wire was worn through in several places—proof of the abrasive quality of a big skate's tough hide.

A strong barrel swivel should be used between trace and reel line. Do not use link swivels for this sort of heavy duty work. The wire link is a weak point which can easily break under strain.

SKATE-FISHING METHODS

For skate and ray of all types and sizes, a running leger is the only practical form of terminal tackle to use. These fish are, by nature of their shape, obviously bottom feeders. To be successful, the bait must therefore be anchored right on the sea bed.

Skate are sluggish, inactive fish which seldom chase after their food, preferring to wander slowly across the bottom picking up any edible object they can find. To work properly, a leger intended for skate fishing should carry enough weight to anchor it in one position. Long flowing traces are not necessary. Most successful anglers use the trace swivel as a stop for the lead (see Fig. 4).

Anglers along the south coast have recently discovered that skate are attracted by the flash of an artificial spoon blade, and some good catches have been taken on normal leger tackle to which a swivelled spoon blade has been added (see Fig. 5). Presumably, the skate see the spoon blade as a small fish, which they attempt to catch, the bait itself being located the moment they drop on to the spoon.

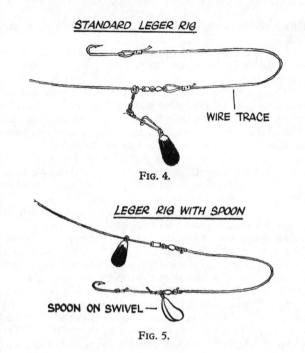

STANDARD LEGER RIG

WIRE TRACE

FIG. 4.

LEGER RIG WITH SPOON

SPOON ON SWIVEL—

FIG. 5.

SKATE BITES

Skate bites follow a very definite pattern. Unfortunately, many anglers have formed the habit of striking at the first indication of a bite. This may be all right as far as many types of fish go, but a premature strike during a skate-fishing session will only lead to a number of lost fish. Patience is the password when skate are the quarry. It is essential to sit back and ignore the preliminary bite indications, so giving the fish time to take the bait right inside its mouth. The first pull on the rod tip is not, in fact, a bite at all; it is just caused by the fish flopping down on top of the bait and the line. A strike at this stage will simply whip the bait out from under the body of the fish and, in all probability, put it off feed for the remainder of the day. To avoid this, the first preliminary bites should be left to develop. Once the fish has the bait well inside its mouth it will move, pulling the rod tip slowly down as it goes.

29

This is the time—and the only time—to attempt to set the hook.

Most of the smaller skates and rays swim with the tide when they move away with the bait. Very big skate usually swim up against the tide causing the line to fall slack as they go. This slackening is a clear indication that the fish can be struck, and also a fair warning that it is a big fish. I have seen several anglers receive this sort of bite from skate in the 100-lb. class, and on each occasion the angler has been puzzled at the sudden lack of weight on the end of his line. Invariably, their first belief is that in some way or another their lead has come off. It is only when they reel up the slack and feel the full weight of the fish that they realise just what they are up against.

Probably the luckiest angler I ever saw was a man fishing off the Hampshire coast who had this type of bite, did not realise what it was and let the fish wind the line twice round the boat's anchor rope. By all the laws of fishing, that should have been the end of the matter; but the line held long enough for the fish to work its way up the rope to the surface. Then, in full view of everyone in the boat, the great fish swam twice round the rope, unwound the line and was gaffed as it cruised past the side of the boat. When weighed, it tipped the scales at exactly 100 lb.—a fine, clean-looking female white skate which should have escaped within seconds of twisting the line around the rope.

Playing a big skate is often a long and exhausting job. First the fish has to be coaxed off the sea bed, then it has to be played against the tide. Under no circumstances should it be allowed to get its head down. If it does, the flow of water pressing down on its angled body, coupled with its own weight and muscle strength, will usually be enough to break the line. In Ireland I have seen several big skate lost right on the surface simply because the angler relaxed for a second or two and gave the fish the opportunity to get its head down. One exhausted fisherman even made the mistake of trying to bring extra pressure to bear on the fish by laying the rod over the gunwale of the boat. This man not only lost his fish but also smashed his rod off at the butt in the process. Probably more rods are broken per annum by big skate than by any other species; but providing an angler is willing to play the fish carefully, these breakages should never occur. A shoulder harness and a belt-type rod bucket are a good investment if

30

you intend to do much serious big skate hunting. Each boat fishing over big skate ground should be equipped with two long-handled heavy-duty gaffs.

A Word of Warning

Do not even attempt to extract the hooks from the mouth of a big skate by hand. The crushing power of the rasp-like lips is enormous and could easily pulp unwary fingers. The

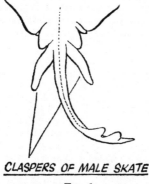

CLASPERS OF MALE SKATE

FIG. 6.

thrashing, spiky tail of a large skate should be avoided: it can inflict a painful blow. Finally, be very careful of the claspers of male skate (see Fig. 6). They contain a sharp, bony plate which can cause a nasty cut.

Although this chapter mainly covers skate and ray fishing, I feel that two other fish are worth including: the monkfish and the angler fish. Both occur frequently on skate ground and are more likely to fall to skate tackle than any other rig.

Monkfish (see page 32)

Monkfish are the missing link between the shark and the skate families. They are often confused with the angler fish, but the two species bear little resemblance to each other. In colour, the monkfish is usually greyish brown, but in Solent waters I have caught several greenish-brown specimens. The average weight of rod-caught monkfish is generally between 25 and 45 lb., but specimens up to 60 lb. are by no means rare. I once examined a monster monkfish that had been caught on a long line by a south Cornish fishing boat. This fish weighed-in at a little over 100 lb. Monkfish have a wide distribution, but are commonest in the southern half of the Channel. Large ones are commonly caught in numbers off the south-west coast of Ireland.

Monkfish are ungainly creatures, incapable of showing any great turn of speed. To catch their food, they have developed the habit of fanning the sea bed vigorously with their fins.

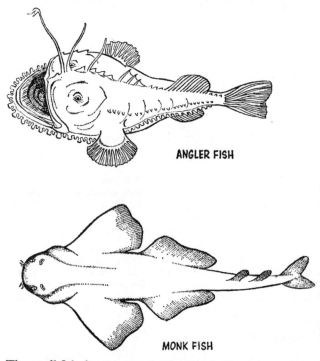

ANGLER FISH

MONK FISH

The small fish that are attracted by the cloudy water provide an easily catchable supply of food. Practically anything small that swims will be eaten by hungry monkfish, but small flatfish seem to form their main diet. They are great scavengers and will eat any dead fish they can find, irrespective of whether or not it is stale or fresh. Many south coast anglers are convinced that the more smelly a bait becomes the more it will attract monkfish.

Despite their large average size and bulky thick-set appearance, monkfish seldom put up much resistance when hooked. I have known the odd specimen to fight really hard, but this is unusual.

Most professionals dislike the monkfish and consider it dangerous to handle. In this respect, I must say I agree with them. A big monk has a formidable set of tooth-filled jaws and the unpleasant habit of suddenly lunging forward, snapping its mouth open and shut as it goes. My advice, then, would be to treat any monkfish you catch with respect. If you have no use for it, get it back alive into the sea as quickly as possible. If necessary, leave the hook in its mouth. A big fish like a monk will soon dispose of a hook, so you will not do it any harm if you cut the trace and lose the hook.

Angler Fish

This fish, occasionally called by the local name 'fishing frog', is probably the ugliest species on the British list. Its huge head and sharply tapering body make it easy to identify. Like the monkfish, it is a spring and summer visitor which spends the cold winter months in deep-water areas well offshore.

Angler fish have a wide distribution and have been recorded from all parts of the British Isles. These ugly, misshapen fish have a tendency to turn up in the most unusual places. Many very large specimens have, in fact, been taken by small-boat anglers fishing for 'flatties' in shallow water.

The angler fish is a confirmed bottom feeder and lives almost entirely on fish. Owing to its grotesque shape, it has to rely on ambushing its food, for it is practically incapable of fast bursts of speed and is therefore unable to pursue and catch its prey. Instead, nature has furnished it with a strip of skin which is attached to the end of the first ray of its dorsal fin. This strip of skin is used as a lure to attract small fish to within striking range of the angler's huge tooth-filled mouth —hence the name angler fish. The fin ray, which acts as a fishing rod, is long enough to be inclined forward right over the fish's mouth, and there can be little or no doubt that the angler activates the lure to make it more attractive to the shoals of food fish.

Very occasionally, the angler will rise to the surface and try to engulf a sleeping sea-bird. Quite recently, two anglers fishing off Bournemouth, Hants, managed to release a live cormorant from the jaws of a really large angler fish.

Like cod, the angler will pick up all sorts of trash from the sea bed and swallow it. Jam jars, tins, sea weights, lumps of scrap metal, corks and bits of wood have all been found in the stomachs of these fish, so it would seem that a hungry angler fish will eat practically anything it can find.

Boat anglers only catch angler fish by accident for, although they are by no means rare, they seem to lead a solitary, nomadic sort of existence. It is unusual to catch more than the very occasional specimen. Most of those that are caught on rod and line fall to baits fished on skate or turbot tackle.

Although it cannot in any way be classed as a true fighting fish, the bulk of a big angler makes it a formidable opponent to tackle. The two that I have caught felt just like weed-filled sacks—and on both occasions I was not at all sure that I had in fact hooked a fish until the creatures surfaced.

CHAPTER II

Tope and Allied Species

THE tope, a small member of the shark family, is very popular with boat anglers in most parts of Great Britain. There is, of course, an official tope club in Britain, and many areas hold annual tope-fishing festivals which are usually very well attended. To become a member of the tope club, it is necessary to catch a tope of over 30 lb. on rod and line. Each year, this club awards a number of trophies for the best fish of the season.

The tope has a typically shark-like appearance with its two dorsal fins and prominent gill slits. Its big tail has a deeply notched upper lobe, and the fish has a grey or greyish-brown back and white underparts. The average weight of rod-caught tope is about 30 lb., but fish of 45 lb. are by no means exceptional. The record rod-caught specimen weighed over 70 lb.— a fair indication that tope can reach a large size. In some areas, tope have been referred to as the 'poor man's shark'— an apt description for a fish that can provide the ordinary angler with all the thrills of shark fishing at a fraction of the cost.

Contrary to popular belief that they are confined to Britain's south and south-western coastlines, tope have a wide dis-

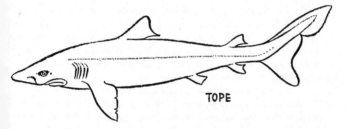

TOPE

tribution. In the Wash they are very common, and some large catches are taken annually from this area. Farther north, they are rarely caught until one gets as far as Scotland. In Luce Bay and around the Scottish islands these fish are often very

35

common, and it would seem likely that they can be caught almost anywhere around Great Britain provided that anglers are prepared to go out and fish properly for them with the right baits and tackle. In recent years, several Welsh ports have consistently made news with tope catches; and in 1969, tope were being caught off Liverpool—proof indeed that these fish are more common than most people imagine them to be.

Tope are a summer species. The best catches are made during the four-month period from June until the end of September. Where I live, on the Hampshire coast, the first tope catches are made about mid-May—June and July being the most productive months. During the past two seasons, however, large tope have been caught during December and January on baits intended for cod. As yet, it is impossible to say whether or not these are 'freak' captures or if in fact the tope are present in the area throughout the whole of the year, for it is only during the last season or so that local boats have gone out regularly after the winter cod. I am fairly sure that time will show some tope do stay close to the shore the whole year round; but until we have had time to go out to the tope grounds regularly during the winter months, this will be difficult to prove conclusively.

Taken on an overall basis, tope can be classed as game fish; for although everyone does encounter the odd specimen that gives up without a struggle, the majority caught on rod and line put up a determined battle before they can be tailed or gaffed into the boat. Probably the best catch of tope ever taken off the Hampshire coast was the one I and a party of friends made during early June 1965. On the day, we had 750 lb. of tope. The smallest fish weighed 32 lb. 9 oz. and the largest 54¼ lb. All the fish were caught less than a mile from the shore, on a mark not 35 ft. deep. Days like this do occasionally occur—but even then, this could be classed as a notable catch of specimen fish

I have also had as many as eight tope to my own rod at Rhyle, but these did not have the high average weight of the Hampshire fish. I once had a boat-fishing holiday at the Scottish port of Fort William, and tope and large dogfish were the only fish of any size that came our way. The tope fishing from this port, and many other similar ports on the west coast of Scotland, has tremendous potential. I have no doubt that, now the Scottish Tourist Board is making an organised attempt to exploit the magnificent Scottish boat-fishing grounds, tope will be caught in ever-increasing numbers by visiting and local anglers alike.

Practically every large tope caught is a female. The males tend to average approximately 30 lb., although I once had one of 45 lb. while boat fishing off Newquay, in north Cornwall. Unfortunately, tope have become increasingly scarce along the south coast in recent years—due, no doubt, to the fact that almost every tope caught in the past has been killed. I never cease to be surprised that anglers who should know better still make a point of destroying each tope they catch in the mistaken belief that they are helping the other fish by killing the predators which feed on them. This shallow thinking is ridiculous to an extreme. Without fish like tope to keep some sort of natural balance, various species of small sea fish quickly overbreed, with the result that they soon exhaust the food supplies of a given area and, being half-starved, become stunted.

A prime example of this are the pouting which have now started to increase at a fantastic rate in many areas where the once plentiful tope-packs have been fished out. In my own area, the Solent is a typical example of this. When tope were plentiful, most of the pouting caught were of a reasonable average size. Since the mass-destruction of Solent tope which took place during the early and mid 1960s, however, pouting have become so numerous that over many marks which once fished well they are the only fish left. With the average size of Solent pouting now down to about 8 in. long, the outlook is poor unless, by some miracle, the Solent tope-packs stage a comeback.

I make a point of returning tope alive to the water whenever possible. Although I have no objection to anglers retaining the odd very large tope for competition purposes, I can see no point in bringing small- and medium-sized tope ashore just to show to friends and neighbours. Far too many of these grand fish finish up in the dustbin or under rose beds. I think it is about time that sea anglers came to their senses and, with an eye to sport in future years, returned the bulk of their tope catches alive to the sea.

TOPE TACKLE

Rods

To get the best out of tope fishing, it pays to fish with as light a rod as possible at all times. Some of the best tope fishermen I have met have been freshwater anglers who have used adapted freshwater tackle for all of their tope fishing. Peter Stone, the well-known angling writer, once showed me a beautiful rod that he had built and designed specifically for tope fishing in Christchurch Bay, Hants. Far longer than the normal run of tope rods, this one was capable of handling lines of up to 20 lb. b.s. Peter used it successfully for tope fishing on many occasions and caught some very good fish on it. To the best of my knowledge, there is only one rod manufactured for all-round tope fishing, designed by Southern ITV's Out of Town man Jack Hargreaves and produced by Davenport and Fordham, the specialist rod builders. This particular rod is made for general tope fishing all round the British Isles and, although it is a little on the heavy side for my liking, it is the most up-to-date boat rod of the tope type at present available.

Reels

As a charter-boat skipper, I used to see a lot of unsuitable tackle used for boat fishing—a typical example being a large fixed spool reel which one man insisted on using. This type of reel is perfectly designed for beach casting and rock or pier fishing, but it has no place in a boat. Unfortunately, the angler in question ignored all my advice and brought this reel out on all his booked trips. Finally, the day came when he hooked a tope, which promptly ran out practically all the line and snapped the bale arm off the reel. The fish was eventually brought to the boat by hauling the line up by hand. Through his own stupidity, the angler had wrecked a perfectly good casting reel by using it for a purpose other than the one for which it was designed. At the same time, he had almost lost the first decent-sized fish he had hooked—proof indeed that to fish properly for a hard-fighting species like tope you must have the correct tackle.

There are, of course, anglers who go to the opposite extreme and turn up with a set of tackle capable of stopping a tuna or a big shark. This, again, is entirely the wrong approach. A medium-sized multiplying reel capable of holding

300 yards or more of 30-lb. b.s. line will do admirably for all aspects of tope fishing. There are many serviceable patterns available, ranging in price from approximately £6 to £12 each. I have recently taken to using the Intrepid 'Buccaneer', which, for a medium-priced reel, has stood up admirably to the thorough testing it has had.

Line

There is no necessity to use extra-strong line for tope fishing. Provided that the reel holds 300 yards of 25- or 30-lb. b.s. line and the star drag·is set correctly, any tope one is likely to encounter round British coasts can be easily beaten. I have had several tope in the 50-lb. class over the years; and although I have known a fish to run out over 150 yards of line during the initial stages of a battle, I have always found that they tend to burn themselves out long before the 200-yard mark is reached and can be easily turned and pumped back to the boat without ever having run out all the reel line. The last tope I caught—a 40 lb. male fish—did not take more than 25 yards of line from the reel at any time during the fight.

From my own experiences with tope, I cannot credit the stories I hear of fish running out 300 yards or more of line without stopping. I can only assume that these reported occurrences are really no more than invented angling stories.

For tope fishing, a braided line is much better than a monofilament line. The stretch in a long length of nylon makes it very difficult to maintain constant contact with a running fish. Braided line does not stretch, so there is no danger of losing contact during the time the fish is pulling against the line.

Hooks and Traces

No two tope fishermen can ever agree on the size of the hook and the length of the trace to use for tope fishing. Some swear by extra long traces, and others are equally convinced that a short trace will suffice.

Choice of hook size depends entirely on the type and size of the bait you intend to use. I am afraid that in this respect most sea anglers lag a long way behind the average freshwater angler, who has learned from an early age that it is essential to use the right combination of bait and hook size at all times. I have often seen sea anglers hooking a whole herring or mackerel on a size 2-0 sea hook in the fond belief that one hook will do for small or large baits.

As a charter-boat skipper, I saw so many large fish lost through this kind of ignorance that I finally made a point of inspecting each man's tackle before he started fishing. In this way, I was able to gently lead my customers round to the right way of angling. I found that once I had explained the reasons for changing hooks to suit different baits, the anglers seldom made the same mistake twice. In consequence, many of them caught plenty of tope and other large fish from my boat.

For small soft baits of the fish fillet or imported squid type, a size 6-0 stainless steel Model Perfect hook is ideal. For whole fish baits, used either alive or dead, an 8-0 or even 10-0 hook should be used. Tope have big mouths—and although a 10-0 hook may look enormous in the hand, it does not look over-big in the mouth of a good-sized tope.

As far as traces go, I would advise any angler to use a trace of 2 to 3 ft. in length. Traces of 5 to 7 ft. may well keep the rough skin of the tope away from the reel line, but they are pretty unmanageable—particularly when made up of nylon-covered wire which, in long lengths, tends to twist and kink with the movement of the bait in the water. I have never lost a tope through using a shortish wire trace, although on several occasions I have lost fish through faulty wire.

BAITS

Tope are bottom feeders but not, in my opinion, scavengers —although they are quite content to pick up an easy meal in the shape of a freshly dead fish or a fish fillet. Most of the tope I have caught have contained mainly flat-fish and small pouting, but in some stomach contents I have found hard-backed crabs and various species of small bottom fish, such as dragonets, sea scorpions, blennies, etc. Tope are also very fond of squid or cuttle-fish. In the Solent area, local anglers say that the first sign of tope being about is when they find cuttle-fish bodies, minus the heads, floating on the surface.

I would say that the vast majority of rod-caught tope fall to either mackerel or herring baits; but almost any small fish can be used for tope catching, my favourite being pouting which I use either alive or dead. During the 1969 season, a number of Solent-caught tope fell to small live bass. Personally, I think it wrong to use fish like bass or mullet for bait when unwanted fish like pouting can be easily obtained. In Scotland, I have caught tope on small haddock, wrasse and gurnard. It therefore seems to me that, providing a bait is fresh, tope are extremely catholic in their tastes. I am sure that if more anglers used live baits for tope fishing far more very big tope would be caught.

Live baits should be hooked once through the wrist of the tail (see Fig. 7). This gives a firm hook-hold without killing

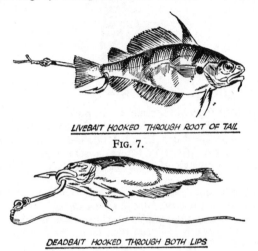

LIVEBAIT HOOKED THROUGH ROOT OF TAIL

FIG. 7.

DEADBAIT HOOKED THROUGH BOTH LIPS

FIG. 8.

the bait. Dead baits can be hooked in a similar fashion or through both lips (see Fig. 8). Fillet baits should be tied to the shank and eye of the hook, otherwise water pressure will cause them to slide down and bunch up on the bend of the hook. A bait that does this will rarely catch tope. A fresh mackerel with the head removed makes a first-class tope bait. The hook should be passed through the wrist of the bait's tail and lashed to the thick end of the bait with thread or wool (see Fig. 9).

HANDLING OF TOPE

Provided that a hooked tope is played out carefully and firmly, it can usually be brought easily up to the side of the

boat. Once there, it is ready to be pulled inboard. At this stage it can be gaffed or tailed, depending entirely on whether it is to be retained or released. Modern-thinking sea anglers with an eye to sport in future seasons now tail most of the tope they catch to avoid damaging them with the gaff point.

Tailing is simple enough if one keeps cool and gets a firm grip on the hard wrist of the tope's big tail. Once this is accomplished and the tail is out of the water, the fish will be practically powerless. It can then be dragged or lifted over the gunwale. To avoid harming the fish in any way whatsoever, it should be lifted by the tail and dorsal fin (see Fig. 10). Failing this, it can be pulled bodily over the side. But this method tends to rupture the fish. The tail and dorsal fin technique is therefore the best method to employ.

Once the fish is safely inboard the hook can be removed or, if it is well inside the mouth, the trace can be cut, leaving the hook embedded in the flesh. The tope can then be weighed, photographed and released intact. It will soon shake the hook out of its mouth—and the loss of one hook is a small enough price to pay for allowing a game fish like the tope to live to fight another day.

If it can be avoided, tope should not be picked up by the tail only. When hanging head down the stomach sometimes drops forward and ruptures so badly that the fish will die, even if it appears to swim off strongly when returned to the water. For weighing purposes, the hook of the spring balance should be carefully inserted in one of the gill slits so that the fish hangs tail downwards. For photographs, the fish should be held supported by both hands. Be careful, however, to

CORRECT WAY TO LIFT TOPE

Fig. 10.

avoid the jaws, which snap automatically every time something touches them. Try also to avoid getting tope slime or blood on clothing. It is almost impossible to remove, and it smells abominably. Gaffed tope should be tied alongside the boat until the blood from the gaff wound stops flowing, otherwise the boat will smell for weeks.

Some people like to eat tope steaks, but these fish cannot really be classed as a very edible species. So my advice is to return all fish caught to the water. During a recent season, I caught an unusual quantity of very small tope. These immature fish should be handled as lightly and as little as possible and put back into the sea the moment the hook is removed.

TOPE-FISHING METHODS

Tope are bottom feeders. Consequently, to be successful, a bait must be presented on or close to the sea bed. A plain running leger is the most practical terminal tackle to use, and

43

this gear probably accounts for over 90 per cent of the tope caught annually. I am convinced that hunting tope are attracted by movement and, to a lesser extent, smell. Because of this, my advice to anglers is to impart as much movement to the bait as possible. Live baits will naturally provide their own movement to help attract the prowling tope.

Dead baits or fish fillet baits, on the other hand, can be fished in several different ways. At present, the most widely used method is to stop the lead 8 or 10 ft. from the bait, using a length of valve rubber on a matchstick hitched to the line as a stop. This will allow the bait to waver about with the tide in an attractive fashion.

When fishing alone or with one or two other anglers, this idea can be enlarged on by lowering the baited hook over the stern of the boat and letting it drift away with the tide for 20 or 30 ft. The lead and sliding tackle should be held in the hand until the required length of line is out, then a stop made from a short length of bicycle valve rubber should be hitched to the line to prevent the weight from sliding down to the trace. Once this stop is in place, the lead can be lowered in the normal way until it reaches the bottom, where the bait is free to flow about in a wide arc beyond the lead. When a fish is hooked and the lead weight comes up against the top ring of the rod, the pressure will cause the valve-rubber stop to double up so that it passes through the eye of the sliding link and releases the lead, which will then slide down to the trace swivel and allow the fish to be brought up on a short length of line. A thin sliver of matchstick can also be used—but it must be thin enough to snap under strain, so that it releases the lead correctly without jamming up the tackle. I find this tackle is most manageable in areas that are not subjected to a fierce tidal run. If there is a heavy tide, an extra large weight may have to be used to hold bottom and this might be too heavy for the stop to function properly. These extra long traces can only be used when there are few anglers in the boat, otherwise bad tangles are inevitable.

An equally effective although not widely used method is to use a 5- or 6-ft. length between hook and weight and trot the bait out over the sea bed so that it covers as much ground as possible. To fish this tackle properly, it is essential to achieve the correct balance of terminal gear. The lead should be just heavy enough to hold bottom and light enough to roll every time the rod tip is lifted and line is allowed to run out. This is the most successful technique to use in strong tides. I use a wire line for this kind of fishing (see Chapter IV) simply because the wire, being heavy in itself, requires only a small lead to sink it. The combination of heavy line and light lead is unbeatable for this kind of tope fishing. The wire has the previously mentioned advantage, of not stretching under strain.

Since I first started to use wire and the rolling leger tackle, my tope catches have shown a marked increase. On one occasion, off the Welsh coast, I had eight good fish when the other anglers in the boat had only three fish between them. I have also had a very good week's sport with this type of tackle off the west coast of Ireland, where tope are plentiful but generally of a small average size. By the end of the week, anglers who had seen the wire line and rolling leger in action were leaving no stone unturned in their attempts to obtain a supply of this line.

TOPE ON ARTIFICIAL BAITS

When a tope pack goes on the rampage, the fish will attack almost any bait-sized object that moves. More than one angler has found out, to his cost, that tope will even strike at a string of mackerel feathers being fished close to the bottom. On the Isle of Wight fishing grounds I have hooked a number of tope while feathering for bait fish; and although the majority have quickly bitten through the nylon trace, I have still managed to boat quite a few good-sized specimens. On all but one occasion, I have found the fish hooked fairly inside the mouth —proof that tope will snap at an artificial lure when they are in a feeding frenzy.

To date, English anglers lag far behind American and northern European fishermen in their knowledge of artificial lures for general sea fishing; and, no one in this country has, to my knowledge, carried out extensive experiments with artificial baits for tope catching. No doubt, during the next decade, an artificial bait revolution will take place. When it does, I am convinced that techniques for catching tope on man-made baits will be devised. Heavy pirk-type jig baits definitely attract tope, for I have had several fish on these lures on marks in Luce Bay, Scotland.

TOPE ON FLOAT TACKLE

Float fishing for tope is a shallow-water boat-fishing method that I have found to work extremely well. This method is only really practicable during slack-tide periods; but when conditions are right, it can be a most rewarding and exciting form of angling. Basically, this method is simply a scaled down adaption of the technique employed to catch shark on float-fished baits—the float, of course, being smaller. I use a flat, white plastic detergent bottle as a float, but there are several large-sized sliding sea floats that are also suitable for this work.

The most important point to remember when setting up this tackle is that tope are bottom feeders, so the bait must be fished either on or just off the sea bed. As an example, let us say that a known tope mark is 30 ft. deep. The float stop should, then, be set at about 5 ft. more than the known depth of water to allow for drag, etc. Under normal circumstances, lead should not be used to weight the bait down. If, however, the tide is running fairly rapidly it is advisable to use a $1\frac{1}{2}$-oz. barrel lead on the line just above the trace swivel (see Fig. 11). This should be sufficient to take the bait down and keep it close to the bottom. In really hard tides it may be

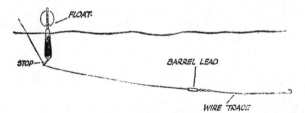

FIG. 11.

necessary to set the float at 15 ft. more than the depth of the water, to allow for additional water pressure on the bait which might tend to lift it off the sea bed. All things being equal, this method can be easily fished from an anchored boat.

A braided line should be used for this style of tope fishing because, being fairly buoyant in itself, it will tend to stay close to the surface as the bait is worked away from the boat. This is important. A sunken line between rod tip and float can lead to all sorts of complications. Bad tangles will be al-

46

most inevitable, and direct striking at a taking fish will become an impossibility due to pressure of water on the sunken line.

When the tide is barely moving, the boat can be allowed to drift so that the bait gradually covers several miles of ground. This is only advisable when the bottom is comparatively snag free, otherwise the bait will continually be caught up on underwater obstructions.

For float fishing for tope, a large bait seems to produce the best results. I usually use a whole mackerel or herring, hooked once through the root of the tail so that it trips along head down over the bottom. A bait presented in this way would seem to appear as a fairly natural object to the tope, for I get more runs on a bait hooked in this fashion than I do on baits hooked in any other way.

Fishing for tope in this manner calls for a considerable amount of concentration. The moment a fish pulls the float under, it is essential to snap the reel out of gear so that the running fish is free to take line as it moves away. Tope do not tend to be timid biters, but they quickly drop a bait if they suspect that there is something wrong with it. Strangely enough, the drag on the float does not appear to worry them; but a slight pull from the rod tip will often cause them to eject the bait immediately.

I find that most of the tope I catch follow a definite pattern. First comes the actual taking of the bait. This is normally a fairly savage affair: it would seem that, as a general rule, the fish actually snap up the bait on the run. Because of this, the float either disappears with a crash or races away over the surface, submerging gradually as it goes. To ensure that there are no snags at this initial stage, it is essential to hold the rod at all times. Once the float has gone and the reel spool is revolving at speed, the angler must not lose his head and attempt to strike until either the fish begins to slow down—which it usually does—or it is obvious that it is not going to stop. In either event, the reel should be put back into gear and, as the line pulls tight, the rod should be lifted steadily back over the shoulder. Heavy strikes should be avoided, otherwise a breakage may occur. By tightening the line and allowing the spring of the raised rod to set the hook, the possibility of snapping the line on the strike is practically eliminated.

Spur-dog

The spur-dog is rather similar in outward appearance to the tope, and many novice anglers confuse the two. Although adult specimens grow to approximately 3½ to 4 ft. in length, this species does not reach the size of the tope. When handling spur-dog, great care should be taken to avoid the claw-like spine on the dorsal fin. It can easily cause a nasty, jagged cut.

Spur-dog are normally found in great packs and are therefore very popular with anglers who specialise in sea-angling competitions; for once a pack is found, the fish can be caught two or three at a time until a large total weight is amassed. From the sporting point of view, however, spur-dog are of little interest to the average angler because they are easy to catch and put up very little fight when hooked. Commercial

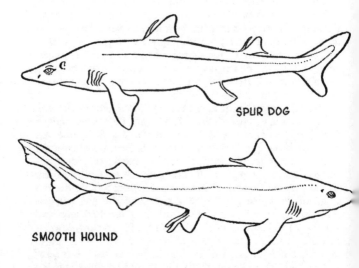

SPUR DOG

SMOOTH HOUND

fishermen loathe them, for spur-dog packs commonly attack and tear open nets to get at the fish inside.

Unlike most of their tribe, spur-dog do not confine their activities to the bottom only. They are quite content to feed at any level as long as they can get an ample supply of food. Voracious to the extreme, a pack of hungry spur-dog will take any bait the angler cares to use—and they tend to strike a bait so savagely that more often than not they hook themselves in the process. The majority of anglers regard them as bait-robbing scavengers. They have a novelty value the first time a pack is encountered, but the continual catching of fish soon begins to pall. Having had one good catch of spur-dog, very few anglers show any great wish to repeat the slaughter.

Although the best way to catch spur-dog is to leger a fish fillet bait, a string of baited mackerel feathers or single- or double-hook paternoster trot rigs can also be used to good effect. Spur-dog will also strike at artificial baits; and in Scottish waters around Caithness I have had some big catches of these fish while using pirk baits for cod, coalfish and pollack.

Smooth-hound

This species probably fights harder than any other member of the dogfish clan. Because of this, and its reputation as a table fish, it is quite popular with boat fishermen. In general appearance, the adult smooth-hound is very similar to a small tope. It does not, however, have the graceful shape of the tope and its fins are rather large in comparison to its body. Adult specimens are grey on the back with white underparts. Immature fish usually have a freckling of white spots on their back. These normally disappear as the fish matures, but I have had large smooth-hound still showing these pale spots.

Two local names for this fish are ray-mouthed dogfish and skate-toothed shark. For positive identification, the mouth of this species quickly gives it away: instead of having proper teeth, its lips are covered with hard slabs like those of a skate or ray.

Smooth-hounds up to $6\frac{1}{2}$ ft. long have been caught by commercial fishermen, and I have seen specimens to over 20 lb. caught on rod and line.

Like most of the dogfish family, the smooth-hound is a confirmed bottom feeder; but unlike other dogfish it rarely eats fish, preferring to feed on worms, crabs, etc. Large smooth-hound are very common in the Solent, where they are usually caught during the summer months on leger tackle baited with either ragworm or hermit-crab tails. On lightish tackle, a large smooth-hound can be relied upon to

49

put up a good struggle before it can be boated. Size for size, its fighting ability is similar to that of the tope.

Smooth-hound are commonest along the south coast, and the only place I have ever caught them myself or heard of them being caught in any quantity is the Solent. They seem to feed best during sultry weather, and most of my largest catches have been made in the late evening. Unlike tope, which are bold biters, smooth-hound normally play with a bait for some time before actually taking it properly into their mouths. Because of this habit, it is advisable to ignore preliminary bite indications and wait till the fish moves away with the bait before attempting to strike—otherwise, in all probability, the strike will only pull the hook and bait out of the fish's lips. A freshly caught smooth-hound makes excellent eating; being boneless, it is easy to clean and cut up.

CHAPTER III

Sea Bream

ALTHOUGH neither of Britain's two common species of sea bream—red and black—grows to any great size, both are game fighters on light tackle. The black bream, in particular, is a most popular fish with south-coast boat anglers. Both species appear to be rather limited in distribution, and northern anglers have little opportunity of catching either fish in their home areas. The red bream is the commonest of the two, but even this fish can only be found in quantity off the south and south-western coasts.

The adult red bream is a handsome deep-bodied fish. Its dorsal fin is long, well-shaped and spiny, and its beautiful pectoral fins are elongated and sickle-shaped. In colour, a mature red bream is orange-red with silvery pink sides. To make identification even easier, it has a distinctive black patch on its shoulder, close to the start of the lateral line. This patch is absent on immature fish. Red bream also have very large eyes.

An average rod-caught red bream weighs between $1\frac{1}{2}$ to $2\frac{1}{2}$ lb., but fish up to almost 8 lb. have been taken. In West Country waters I have taken many large red bream during the day while bottom fishing in deep water. Basically, however, the red bream is a nocturnal feeder which bites best after dark. Strangely enough, these fish, which are normally bottom feeders, often rise towards the surface during the late evening. I have caught many while driftline fishing just under the surface. Small red bream live mainly on shellfish, but the larger specimens eat almost any small thing that swims.

Some time ago, huge shoals of red bream invaded St. Austell Bay annually and it was not unusual to go out in a small boat for an evening's fishing and return after two or three hours with a hundredweight or more of plump medium-sized fish. In recent years, however, the vast shoals have stopped coming to the area. The cause may be due to over-fishing but the increased flow of china clay waste into the bay may have something to do with it.

Although red bream are beautiful fish, they cannot compare in fighting spirit with black bream. Unfortunately, black bream have a very limited distribution. Although the odd fish or two can be caught from any rough-ground mark in the Channel, the main shoals are strictly localised along one short section of the Sussex coast. Littlehampton is, without doubt, the best-known black bream centre in the country. Charter boats working from this port tend to specialise in bream fishing during the spring and early summer months. But black bream have suffered badly from over-fishing in recent years, and even at Littlehampton immense catches are now rarely taken—although at one time it was common for a single boat to land several hundredweight of big bream each time it went out.

In shape, black bream are very similar to the red bream. The pectoral fins, however, are not as long. As its name implies, the black bream is a dusky fish. The basic body colour is dark bluish-grey, and the underparts are silvery white. Fish which live on really rough ground often have dark vertical bands down their sides. I caught some very distinctly striped black bream while fishing a mark off Hengistbury Head, Hants, several years ago. Fish from a nearby ground known as Boscombe Rough, however, are often without obvious stripes—proof that bream adapt their colour scheme to suit the ground they inhabit.

Small shoals of good-sized black bream can occur in the most unlikely places. I had five fine specimens while pollack fishing on a mark to the east of Fowey Harbour, on ground where black bream had never been seen before. The area between Freshwater Gate and St. Catherine's Lighthouse on the Isle of Wight has produced some fine black bream catches during the past two seasons. I had 18 fish from this area on one occasion, and other similar catches have been made over the same ground. This whole area is practically virgin water as far as boat fishing is concerned; and it is just possible that it could be a black bream hot-spot, for in terms of sea miles it is not very far from the Kingmere Rocks off Littlehampton —most famous of all the Sussex black bream marks.

Black bream never reach the size of red bream, although fish of between 3 and 4 lb. are common along the Sussex coast. But as a fighting species the black bream, as previously mentioned, is far superior to the red bream. Even a medium-sized specimen will put up a magnificent fight on all but the

52

heaviest of tackle. The food of the black bream is similar to that of the red bream in all respects.

Like all south-coast boat anglers, I am hoping that new black bream hot-spots will be discovered during the next few seasons. It would be a great pity if such a fine fighting species should gradually become a rarity through anglers over-fishing a particular area and killing too many stock fish in the process. I am hopeful that the black bream will stage a comeback. Red bream did this some years ago, at a time when everybody assumed that they were on the verge of extinction. Now they swarm again in large numbers. With luck, the black bream will reappear in similar quantity.

TACKLE

Sea bream are essentially light tackle fish. Unfortunately, many anglers still go out to fish bream grounds with heavy-weight gear, giving the fish little opportunity of showing their true fighting ability. My advice to anglers who wish to enjoy their bream fishing is to use only the lightest of boat rods. My own rod is the Abu Fladden, which I use with a small multi-plier loaded with 12-lb. line. A good-sized red or black bream hooked on this outfit puts up a magnificent fight.

For the angler wishing to fish even lighter than this, a pike or salmon spinning rod used with a multiplier or centre-pin real and 8- to 10-lb. line is the rig to use. This ultra-fine tackle is best used in uncrowded boats, for a long rod and light line can quickly cause unnecessary confusion in a crowded vessel.

Hook sizes for black or red bream fishing should range from size 1 to 8 (freshwater scale). Both types of fish have small mouths and, with light tackle, a big hook would be difficult to set when the strike is made.

BOATING SEA BREAM

The only practical way of bringing sea bream into a boat is with a medium-sized landing net. This is simple to use and allows unwanted fish to be returned unharmed to the sea.

CONSERVATION OF BLACK BREAM

Huge catches of large black bream are now an unusual event, mainly because anglers who should have known better

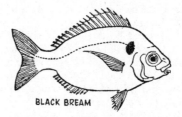

BLACK BREAM

were guilty of taking far too many fish home with them. If the black bream shoals are to be given a fighting chance of re-establishing themselves, present-day boat anglers must be prepared to set themselves personal limits. Six 2-lb. bream, for example, are enough for any fisherman to take at one time. Surplus fish should be returned immediately they are caught.

Unfortunately, it is easy to forget such limits in the excitement of catching one good fish after another; but to finish up at the end of the day with two or three dozen dead bream is an unforgivable act. So please have consideration for the future and return any fish which you do not need as food for yourself or others.

METHODS

Black bream shoal and feed at different levels at varying stages of the tide. At slack water, for example, they are usually feeding right on the bottom; but as the tide starts to run, they normally rise up to the surface. Red bream, on the other hand, stay right on the bottom during the day and only start to rise to the surface as night begins to fall.

For both species, a plain running leger is the best type of terminal tackle—but in the case of the black bream it should incorporate an extra-long flowing trace. As a rough guide, the length of the trace should equal the length of the rod: an 8-ft. rod with an 8-ft. trace, and so on.

Heavy leads should be avoided when bream are the quarry. On many occasions, while fishing with extra-fine lines, I have found I can touch bottom easily with a $\frac{1}{2}$- to $\frac{3}{4}$-oz. weight. Obviously, the strength of the tidal run in an individual area will dictate the amount of lead to be used, but with fine lines it is seldom necessary to employ more than two or three ounces on any of the known bream grounds.

The lead should be allowed to run freely on the line, being stopped only by the small swivel used to connect the line with the trace. For red bream, it is best to hold the tackle in one place for as long as possible; but for black bream, a moving bait catches the most fish. I catch most of my black bream by letting the tackle down until the lead touches bottom, then retrieving it slowly until either a fish takes the bait or the tackle breaks surface.

Both species of bream are bold biters, but the black bream is a real rod-tip rattler. It is advisable to ignore the first few tugs and wait until the bream actually pulls the rod over and holds it over before striking.

The most generally used baits for bream fishing are ragworm, lugworm, fish strips or mussels. Long strips of squid and whole small sand-eels can also be used. At Littlehampton, it was once common for black bream anglers to use cooked rice grains. I have no record of this particular bait being used elsewhere, but it might be well worth trying on a productive black bream mark.

PATERNOSTER

A light paternoster can be used to catch both species of bream. It should be made up with a 3-ft. trace (see Fig. 12). I find I get more results with the paternoster when I bump it up and down over the bottom by lifting the rod tip and letting out a few yards of line at the same time. The paternoster can be made to work well astern of the boat, and bites will often occur when it is actually on the move.

FLOAT FISHING

In West Country waters I have had many large catches of red bream while float fishing in comparatively shallow water. I have also used this technique on several occasions while black bream fishing off Littlehampton, and find that it works well for both species. The float I use takes 1 to $1\frac{1}{2}$ oz. of lead, which is sufficient to hold the bait down during the slack part of the tide or during most stages of a full neap tide. Normally, I set the tackle so that the lead is about a foot off the bottom. The float is, of course, a slider which is stopped on the line by means of a piece of rubber band. To avoid the stop from becoming wedged in the centre tube of the float, it is advisable to run a small shirt button on to the line between float and rubber stop (see Fig. 13).

Bream bite extremely well on float tackle; and although one is likely to miss many bites while using this technique, the sight of a bright float disappearing abruptly from sight makes

NYLON PATERNOSTER

Fig. 12.

it a most enjoyable experience. Both species of bream fight well, and on light tackle there can be no question of hauling them to the surface. A big bream lunging suddenly for the bottom can easily smash light tackle, so the angler is well advised to give line each time a fish makes a downward plunge.

Expert black bream fishermen sometimes fish with fresh-water trotting rods and 5-lb. line. To control a big bream on tackle as light as this calls for considerable skill. I would not advise the novice angler to try his luck with it until he has

STOP

SHIRT BUTTON

SLIDING FLOAT

FIG. 13.

caught a fair number of big sea bream on the heavier tackle described above.

GROUNDBAIT

Black bream respond well to groundbait. Many charter-boat skippers who fish black bream marks make a habit of attaching a fine-mesh bag full of mashed-up fish flesh to the anchor rope, just above the anchor chain, before dropping it over the side. In slack tides, further groundbait can be mixed up into heavy solid balls and dropped over the side at regular intervals. One successful black bream angler I know uses a combination of minced fish offal, cooked rice and bran to make up his groundbait 'bombs'. This odd mixture obviously works, for its originator catches far more than his fair share of good big bream. At a pinch, almost any mixture—provided that it contains a percentage of fish scraps or pure fish oil—could be used as groundbait for bream fishing, and there is clearly great scope for serious experimentation in this particular field.

CHAPTER IV

Cod, Whiting, Haddock and Pouting

COD are the main quarry of winter boat fishermen. The first fish of the season generally put in an appearance during late September or early October. It is interesting to note that, during the last five seasons, migrating cod shoals have gradually begun to extend their range. For example, cod used to be caught only rarely off Hampshire or Dorset; now, they are very common in these areas and becoming more numerous each season. Farther west still, cod are beginning to show up along the south Devon and Cornish coasts in areas where they have never been caught before. These fish have, of course, always been very common in the eastern section of the English Channel and also in the North Sea. At one time, every keen cod angler travelled to Deal or Dover to catch them. But now that the fish have extended their range, other areas are producing very big cod in such vast numbers that cod fishing has become an extremely popular sport.

If I were asked which area I would consider best for cod fishing, I would undoubtedly choose the western end of the Solent—for although really gigantic catches of cod are still unusual on the grounds off the Isle of Wight, the average size of the fish caught is probably greater than anywhere else in the British Isles. Cod of 20 lb. are commonplace off the island, and the largest cod yet caught in the area tipped the scales at 40 lb. 8 oz. Nine out of the 12 largest cod caught during the 1969–70 season came from this area; and during the period from the beginning of November until mid-December, my own rod accounted for exactly 20 fish over and above the coveted 20-lb. mark.

During the previous season, I was fortunate enough to take part in the largest-ever recorded catch of cod around the Isle of Wight—20 fish with the staggering total gross weight of 450 lb. Only one fish weighed under 20 lb. that day, and we boated six fish of over 30 lb. That day we were fishing from the famous charter boat *Bonito II*—the boat that has starred in so many television angling programmes. Two days

58

after making this catch, we went out to the same grounds to make a successful cod-fishing film.

Cod have always been eagerly sought after by boat anglers; but since the fish have changed their habits and extended their range they are the most popular and most sought-after winter sea fish on the British lists. At present, the cod record stands at a little over 53 lb.; but fish of greater weight exist in our waters, and it can only be a matter of time before a new record is brought to the gaff.

From the boat angler's point of view, cod have much to recommend them. Even a small cod is a largish fish, and a big one is truly enormous. More important still is the fact that cod of any size, provided that they are in good condition,

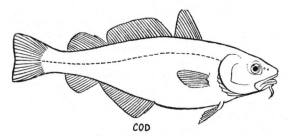

COD

make excellent eating. So the average boat angler who goes out at a cost of around 30s. per day naturally feels that by catching a cod or two he is getting his money's worth—in terms of sport and edible value.

Basically, a cod is not a pretty fish. Its huge head, pot-belly and tapering cylindrical body give it an ugly, ungainly appearance. Even so, a big one fresh from the sea and in the very pink of condition has a peculiar attraction all of its own.

In terms of fighting ability, cod do not rate very highly. Although their bulk and obvious strength make them difficult to pump up from any depth of water, they rarely show any spirit and are usually content to plug round right under the boat. There are exceptions, of course. I can remember one particular day when we caught five cod ranging from 20 to 37½ lb. from a mark a mile outside the Needles Lighthouse, and each fish fought like a tope. But such behaviour is unfortunately rare.

FEEDING HABITS

By nature, cod are bottom feeders. They tend to live in fairly deep water, where they will eat practically anything that comes their way. I never cease to be amazed at the rubbish I find in the stomach contents of cod I catch. This has included large stones, odd bits of metal or wire, bottle tops, paper, bones and white plastic cups of the kind dumped into the sea in their thousands from car ferries and cruise ships. On one occasion I even saw a complete beer-can taken from a large cod. The plastic cups are a common find, and on my last cod-fishing trip of 1969 I had a fish which came to the surface with a cup in its mouth. When it was gutted another was found in its stomach.

As far as natural food is concerned, anything that swims, crawls or sticks to the sea bed and is small enough to eat becomes fair game to the ever-hungry cod shoals. One fish I caught recently had two whole edible crabs inside it, each crab measuring approximately 5 in. across the back.

GROWTH

As I said earlier in this chapter, I am confident that fish of at least 50 lb. in weight exist in fair numbers off Britain's coasts. From checking commercial records, I find that the largest cod ever caught weighed 211½ lb., and Icelandic trawlers still catch cod of over 100 lb. But I am quite certain that cod of this size will never be taken anywhere around the British Isles. Boat anglers who spend their holidays in Iceland do, of course, stand a chance of hooking the odd extremely big fish. At the time of writing, a new cod record has been established with a specimen weighing 46 lb. ½ oz. caught from the Firth of Clyde on a pirk bait.

COD TACKLE

Rods

Almost any strong solid or hollow glass boat-rod can be used to catch cod; but for the angler really wishing to take cod fishing seriously, I advise a more specialised tool. Unfortunately, most rod manufacturers in Britain still seem to believe that the maximum length of a boat rod should be 6½ ft. This is the most easy length to handle in a boat. Although a rod of this length is serviceable, a good cod-fishing rod should be at least 6 in. longer. There are a few enlightened rod builders who have recognised the need for longer rods, but the rods produced by these firms are expensive, costing about £15. However, this is a 'do-it-yourself' age, and good-quality hollow-glass rod blanks can be purchased at reasonable prices. Therefore, the home-handyman can produce his own super de luxe boat rods at approximately half the cost of the shop-bought rod.

When purchasing glass blanks, it is essential to give some thought to what you will require, for a great advantage in building your own rods is that you can choose exactly the fitting you personally desire. My own cod rod, for example, has a steep taper and a test curve of around 10 lb.—which means that it will handle lines of from 25- to 50-lb. b.s. The steep taper gives plenty of progressive power to the rod, yet the actual tip is thin enough to transmit the tiniest bites. The rod also has a roller tip ring and heavy steel guide rings. The roller is a vital essential, for it allows me to use nylon, braided or wire lines as I wish. A rod fitted with an ordinary tip ring would be useless for fishing with metal line due to the constant line kinks, which a roller tip automatically straightens out as the tackle is being retrieved. A boat rod should be bought or designed for the reel you intend to use with it. This is important. A badly matched set of tackle can make constructive angling very difficult and unpleasant.

REELS

A medium-sized multiplier is ideal for cod fishing, although some experts prefer to use a reel of the very large diameter centre-pin type. Personally, for ease and general usefulness, I do not think you can better the multiplier. Make sure, when buying one of these reels for boat fishing, that it is fitted with a metal or fibre-glass spool that will not crack under stress. Nylon line, in particular, tends to contract under pressure; and a reel with a plastic spool will soon become unserviceable when used against heavy fish, like cod. My own cod reels are an Intrepid Buccaneer, a Garcia 624 and a Penn Super Mariner. The first two are loaded with nylon line, and the Penn holds metal line.

61

Medium-sized multiplying reels are, of course, legion and the average tackle shop stocks a dazzling array ranging in price from £4 to £20. Make sure that the reel you buy is backed by a fast and efficient after-sales service. Many of the reels available are of foreign origin and are very good indeed; but I must admit that I do not, as a general rule, like Japanese fishing tackle. At face value, it appears to offer extremely good value for money—but in my experience it does not stand up well in use. Moreover, the Japanese are continually changing models, and I find it difficult to get spare parts for reels more than a year or two old. Believe me, the cod may not be a great fighter, but its sheer bulk makes it a real tackle-tester. My experience is that Japanese tackle just will not take this kind of punishment like English, French, Swedish or American equipment.

LINES

For cheapness, nylon lines provide unbeatable value; but for general reliability, braided lines are preferable despite the fact that they are much more expensive. For general cod fishing, a 30- or 35-lb. b.s. line is best, although more experienced anglers often fish much lighter in an attempt to get some sport from the cod they catch.

Cod are often caught in strong tides. To fish successfully in a heavy tide, the bait must be presented on or very close to the sea bed. This means that you fish either with a nylon or braided line which needs a very heavy lead to hold it down, or you fish with an all-metal line which, being thinner, creates less water resistance than the other lines and, being heavier in itself, sinks by its own weight, so enabling you to fish with very light leads. An example of this is the area in which I do most of my cod hunting. Normally—even on neap tides—there is a heavy run of water through the area which means I have to fish with a weight of from 1 to $2\frac{1}{2}$ lb., just to hold bottom. With wire, however, I can hold over the same ground with 4 to 6 oz. on a neap tide or 8 to 10 oz. on a full spring tide. Because of this, I tend to use wire line for practically all my cod fishing.

The only wire lines readily available are Monel metal and Tidecutter. The latter is stainless and less than half the thickness of Monel metal of the same breaking strain. Being thinner and more flexible, it packs down on the reel spool better than Monel, which tends to be very springy.

Many cod anglers buy metal line, use it once, then discard it as useless or unmanageable. I can understand how they feel. Unless you use a rod fitted with a roller tip ring that works, and also make absolutely certain that you guide the wire back on to the reel spool with the ball of the thumb, it does tend to kink up and bunch on the reel. Some anglers use a leather thumbstall to protect their skin from the metal line. I have never found this to be essential, but it can save blisters if you intend to fish on two or three consecutive days.

I am sure wire is the line of the future. Although it is a little more difficult to control than nylon or braided line, it can be mastered; and for general cod and other fishing in areas where strong tides prevail, it is the obvious way of beating the excess lead problem. Bites registered on wire are much more definite than bites registered on any other kind of line, mainly because the wire enables you to keep in direct contact with the lead and bait (see Fig. 14). With nylon or braided lines a bow is almost inevitable (see Fig. 15); consequently, it is very difficult, if not practically impossible to remain in contact with the terminal tackle except at dead slack water.

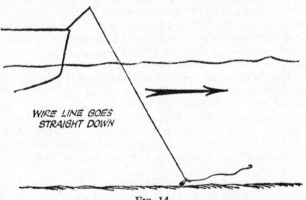

WIRE LINE GOES STRAIGHT DOWN

FIG. 14.

Hooks and Terminal Tackle

Cod of any reasonable size have huge mouths. A fifteen-pounder, for example, could swallow a 3-lb. whiting with no

63

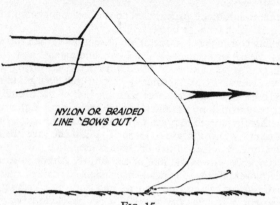

NYLON OR BRAIDED
LINE 'BOWS OUT'

FIG. 15.

trouble at all. Because of this, I consider big hooks to be absolutely essential for cod fishing from boats. Even a bunch of lugworm should be presented on a size 4-0, and larger baits—like squid or fish fillets—require 6-0 or 8-0 hooks to hold them in place.

Although not a hard fighter, the cod is a heavy fish which often lives in deep water and fast tides. When choosing hooks for cod fishing, it is therefore advisable to take these points into account and select them with an eye to their strength as well as their size. My own favourite cod hooks are the flat forged bronzed hooks manufactured by Mustad Ltd. These can be obtained in any good tackle shop and are remarkably cheap to buy. Remember, however, that sharp hooks cannot be bought in tackle shops, so each hook you buy should be carefully sharpened both before and during use. Cod hooks should be razor sharp, for the inside of a cod's mouth tends to be bony and a blunt hook will lose you fish after fish. I make a point of touching up the point of my hook after each fish I catch; and I always examine it carefully after each drop down to see if the point has been turned over as the bait has rolled over the sea bed.

Cod can be caught on plain nylon traces, but it is best to use a trace made up of a length of nylon-covered wire which has the same breaking strain as the reel line. I advocate the use of wire because a big cod has a number of pads of short sharp teeth in its mouth, and its gill rakers are also armed. Wire makes it almost impossible for a hooked fish to escape by chafing through the actual trace. A nylon trace can, of course, be easily severed, and a chafed trace could easily lose you a record-breaker.

Cod traces of nylon-covered wire should be made up in 2-ft. lengths with a swivel at one end and the hook at the other. The wire can be welded instead of crimped, and if welding is done carefully the join will never tear apart in use and should stand up to the strain of pumping big cod up to the surface without effort. I have seen a cod of just under 40 lb. brought to the gaff on a trace made of 30-lb. nylon-covered wire which had been properly welded and which showed no sign of weakening whatsoever.

Welding covered wire is a simple enough operation. First the hook or swivel should be threaded on to the wire, then the wire should be doubled up and wound round itself. An open flame should then be passed over the join until the nylon melts and fuses together to form the actual weld (see Fig. 16). This job can be done at sea with an ordinary match; but to make a really good join, the wire should be welded at home and thoroughly tested when it has had time to cool off.

METHOD OF WELDING NYLON COVERED WIRE

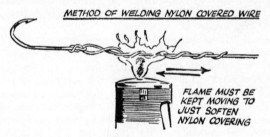

FLAME MUST BE KEPT MOVING TO JUST SOFTEN NYLON COVERING

FIG. 16.

METHODS AND BAITS

Cod are basically a bottom-dwelling species so, whichever method is used, the bait must be presented on or very close to the sea bed. For fishing in areas where cod are numerous and of a fairly low average size, a two- or three-hook pater-noster trot (see Fig. 17) is probably the most killing method to use. It is a fairly sensitive rig which is best fished in areas that are not subjected to fast runs of tide. This style of angling is usually practised from an anchored boat, but I have found

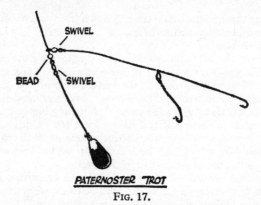

PATERNOSTER TROT

FIG. 17.

it also works well from a drifting craft. The second and third hooks should be weighted by a couple of largish split shot. This will help to stop them winding back around the main hook trace and causing a bad tangle.

The paternoster trot is designed mainly for catching codling and is therefore best used with smallish baits—bunched lug or ragworms, fish or squid strips and shellfish being the best baits to employ.

When fishing over marks where very large cod are known to exist, it is best to use a single-hook leger. Multi-hook tackle may well attract two or more big fish at a time, and a bunch of good cod hooked together will inevitably smash the line almost as soon as they feel the pressure of the rod tip.

At one time cod were regarded as stupid, slow fish which could be lugged out on any rubbishy terminal tackle the winter boat specialist cared to employ. This outlook was probably the main reason why a 32-lb. cod held the record for this species for over 30 years. Modern anglers, fortunately, discovered that by putting considerable thought into cod fishing it was possible to catch dozens of fish over the weight of the old record specimen. Now, each season sees cod to 40 lb.-plus being caught—and fish of up to 35 lb. have come to be regarded as very good but not really outstanding catches.

Nine out of every ten big cod are, at present, taken on a single-hook running leger. The real secret of catching big cod consistently is the ability to accurately judge the length of trace to use on a given day. This length varies considerably. Only continual practice and applied experience can tell you just what to use each time you go out. As a basis, however, I would advise the newcomer to cod fishing to start by leaving a distance of 5 ft. between lead and hook. A simple valve rubber stop attached to the reel line by a couple of half-hitches should be used to stop the lead weight from sliding down to the trace swivel. The lead, of course, is best used clipped directly to a plain Kilmore link, which should be threaded on to the line with a single large plastic bead at either side of it so that it can slide freely at all times. The beads will stop the Kilmore from jamming. The shape of the lead used really depends on whether you want the baited tackle to stay in one place or to roll slowly over the sea bed. For static work, a flat or pyramid-shaped lead should be used; but when rolling the bait out a bomb-shaped lead is better. See Fig. 18.

Nowadays, I find that I catch most of my big cod on extra long traces and I normally use a trace length of 12 ft., for I believe that big cod are attracted to a bait which is fairly free

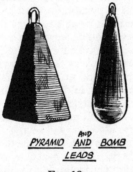

PYRAMID AND BOMB
LEADS

FIG. 18.

to move about with the flow of the tide. Again, I rarely find it necessary to employ a static leger. The majority of the cod I catch are taken well astern of the boat on rolling leger tackle. For this sort of fishing, a wire line is ideal. As it allows the use of a light weight, I find it easier to work the tackle out yard by yard over the sea bottom, thoroughly searching out the fish as it goes.

When a wire line is used for this rolling leger technique it is essential to use a nylon leader on which the leger can run. A weight attached to the actual wire will often jam up in use due to the wire kinking. This does not occur when a nylon leader is used (see Fig. 19). The leader should be at least 6 ft. in length and should be joined to the wire reel line by a small, strong swivel. Never tie the nylon directly to the wire. If you do, a break will be inevitable.

FIG. 19.

The rolling leger method is very simple to use. First the tackle should be sent down to the bottom, as close under the boat as possible. Then, by lifting the rod tip and at the same time releasing the reel spool so that 2 to 3 yards of line run out, the lead can be bounced along the sea bed, away from the boat. By repeating this process at regular intervals, the tackle can be worked steadily over the bottom. With wire line, which allows you to remain in direct contact with the terminal tackle, it is possible to work out the bait for 150 yards or more and still be able to detect bites. I have never successfully achieved this distance with any other type of line.

This form of angling calls for absolute concentration at all times. It is impossible to lay the rod down and still fish the rolling leger properly; and to be successful, the rod must be held wherever the bait is in the water. The static leger is, of course, a less exacting style of angling, well suited to the angler who does not wish to work hard for his fish. A comparison of catches, however, will soon show that the rolling leger is the technique which produces the most fish.

Probably the finest cod bait available to the boat angler is small white Californian squid. These are imported in vast numbers and retail at approximately 25p per pound. A 5-lb. box should be enough to keep three anglers in bait for a whole day's cod fishing. These squid, which average 6 to 7 in. in length, can be used whole or they can be cut up. I find that by breaking off the head section of a squid and cutting the end of the body mantle into strips (see Fig. 20), I hook a larger percentage of cod bites than I did when I used squid whole.

Probably the main attraction of the imported squid is its whiteness, which must show up very well in the water. To add to the attractiveness of the bait, I often use it in conjunction with two dead sprats hooked once through the eye

SQUID MANTLE
WITHOUT HEAD
& CUT INTO
STRIPS

FIG. 20.

socket. These should hang on either side of the squid and act as flashers to attract the attention of the prowling cod shoals (see Fig. 21). There can be no doubt whatever that cod hunt as much by sight as by smell or feel, for a bright bait will catch far more fish than a drab one. On some occasions when the fish are slow to bite, an attracter spoon can be added to the trace (see Fig. 22). The best spoon for this work is an Abu Rauto, which will flash well as it moves with the tide but will not twist the trace up by revolving. I have had many good cod by using this leger/spoon combination, and I feel that there is much to learn about the reaction of cod to artificial lures.

SPRATS USED AS
FLASHERS ON
EITHER SIDE
OF SQUID

FIG. 21.

"FLASHER" SPOON ATTACHED TO COD TACKLE

Fig. 22.

ARTIFICIAL BAITS

Cod of all sizes are confirmed predators, and fishermen in many parts of the world make their living by jigging for cod with shiny lead lures covered in sharp hooks. In commercial fishing circles these baits are known as 'rippers'—a very apt name, for half of the fish caught on them are foul-hooked. Naturally, anglers are not interested in catching cod in quantity by foul means, but adapted—and acceptable— versions of the commercial ripper baits can be used very successfully for everyday cod fishing.

Scandinavian anglers have brought the use of artificial lures for cod fishing to a fine art and regard them as the premier cod-fishing bait. British anglers have not, as yet, begun to experiment to any extent with these baits, but I feel it will not be long before they become the accepted lure for cod fishing in Britain. A season or two ago, one man fishing off the Kent coast boated over 500 lb. of big cod in a single day —and every one of these fish fell to an artificial bait. I know personally of one charter-boat skipper at Lymington, Hants., who advises all the cod anglers he takes out to use jigging baits, and he has caught cod to 34 lb. on these baits.

Most of the cod jigs available in Britain come from Scandinavia. They are the famous pirk baits (see Fig. 23) produced by Abu of Sweden. At present, the heaviest pirk available in quantity is one weighing 7½ oz., but baits up to 1½ lb. can sometimes be obtained. Pirk baits are normally used tied directly to the end of the reel line. I find they work best when attached to a wire line, for the weight of the line tends to hold them close to the bottom no matter what the state of the tide happens to be. Pirk baits are worked on a jigging principle by raising and lowering the rod tip so that the bait continually rises off the sea bed and then drops back again with a fluttering motion.

Shop-bought pirks are fitted with large-sized treble hooks

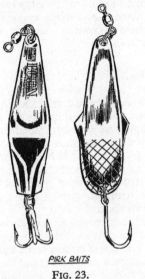

PIRK BAITS

FIG. 23.

which I prefer to remove, substituting instead a 6-0 single hook. My reason for this is that I find the treble hook tends to foul-hook far too many fish, whereas most of the fish I take on a bait fitted with a single hook are caught fair and square inside the mouth.

Pirks can be used as they are or they can be baited. I have caught fish with them in either condition; but for consistent catches a baited pirk is best. Almost anything can be used as bait. The cod do not appear to be at all fussy. I have seen cod taken on pirks baited with squid, worms, fish strip and whelks. The size of the pirk you use depends entirely upon the type of ground and the size of fish you have to contend with. In areas where codling are plentiful, small lures are probably best; but when very big cod are known to exist in an area, my advice would be to use the largest pirk baits you can buy.

Cod tend to take a pirk bait savagely — often hooking themselves firmly in the process. They also put up more fight than fish hooked on leger or paternoster trot tackle, probably due to the fact that they do not have to fight the weight of the lead as well as the constantly applied rod pressure.

Artificial jigging lures of the pirk type are simple enough to construct at home. The average angler should have little trouble in designing his own at a fraction of the cost of the shop-bought varieties.

COD FEATHERS

Basically, cod feathers are an enlarged version of the standard mackerel feathers—although cod seem to prefer a lure made out of plain white hackle feathers, whereas mackerel flies are often dyed bright colours. Cod feathers can be easily and quickly made at home by lashing a bunch of long white turkey hackles to a size 6-0 hook. To ensure that the lashing does not unravel during use, it is advisable to thoroughly cover the thread with two coats of Durofix or similar fast-drying adhesive compound.

A string of cod feathers should contain only two or three lures. When cod are shoaling thickly it is quite possible to hook more than one fish at a time, and a string of more than three feathers can lead to rapid disaster. More important still, a big cod or two lashing about on deck will cause any loose feathers to fly about, which could be dangerous to anyone who happened to be within range of the flailing hooks. I only feather for cod when I fish areas noted mainly for fish of medium size, for two or three decent codling hooked at one time can provide first-class sport on ordinary boat tackle. On big fish ground, I either dispense entirely with feathers or fish just one. In this way, I can be certain of being able to handle any fish that takes the lure.

COD AND TIDE CHANGE

It is still a general belief among anglers in Britain that the optimum time for cod fishing is at the top or bottom of the tide—in other words, the slack- or dead-water period. This is, without a shadow of doubt, a fallacy brought about in the first place because many anglers find it difficult to fish when the tide is actually on the move, the only time they can fish properly being during the change-over period, when the tackle is straight up and down over the side of the boat. I do not doubt for a moment that cod can be taken during the dead-water time; but carefully kept records of catches made in my area during the past three winter cod seasons have shown that eight out of every ten cod caught are taken during the time when the tide is running up or down. Slack-water fish are, in fact, fairly rare catches, and sport often drops right off as the dead-water period approaches. As soon as the tide begins to move again, the fish come on the feed and, as a rule, can be caught steadily throughout the ebb or flood tide. This applies to hard spring tides as well as to slack neap tides.

I am afraid English anglers are still tied too much to tradition for their own good. The sooner they begin to realise that many of the old-wives' tales that are still applied to angling are little more than traditional rubbish the sooner they will begin to catch good fish in consistent numbers. Laziness is, of course, the main problem to overcome. Rather than try to fish properly in a hard tide, far too many people are content to leave the rod propped up over the stern of the boat to fish for itself. An unattended rod seldom catches fish mainly because—unless the angler is prepared to release a few yards of line every few minutes—the pressure of water on a tight line will soon lift the bait and lead up off the sea bed and cause it to kite up and hang suspended well above the bottom. In this condition it does not catch fish, but furthers the nonsensical belief that cod and other species can seldom be caught before or after the slack-water period. The angler who is prepared to apply constructive thought will soon find that fish are there to catch provided that he is willing to work for them. After all, boat fishing can be expensive—so why pay £1·50 or more just to fish for an hour or so at slack water when you can catch fish at any stage of the tide?

Whiting

If the whiting grew to the size of its near relative the cod, it would be a really sporting fish to catch on rod and line, for its streamlined body and rather pointed head give it a much greater turn of speed than the cod. Unfortunately the average whiting caught in Britain weighs somewhere between 1½ to 2 lb. Fish of double this weight can be regarded as large specimens. The largest whiting I have ever taken weighed exactly 4½ lb. and was caught, strangely enough, on a day when I was out trying to catch large whiting for a television programme. If I remember rightly, we caught well over 150 lb. of large whiting that day, which included half a dozen or more fish of over the 4-lb. mark.

It is only necessary to take a close look at the tooth-filled mouth and streamlined body of the whiting to realise that these fish are obviously true predators. They live by preying almost exclusively on small fish of many kinds. Whiting have a very wide distribution and can be caught almost anywhere from one end of the country to the other. This, coupled with their obvious value as a table fish, makes them very popular with the average sea angler, who likes to go home at the end of the day with a catch that he can eat and enjoy.

Basically, whiting, like cod, are a winter species; but boat anglers who can fish deep marks well offshore often catch large bags of good-sized whiting during the summer and autumn months.

Although small live fish form the principal diet of whiting, these greedy fish often resort to bottom feeding as well. Because of this, they can be caught on almost any natural bait the angler can procure. Big whiting can be caught in quantity if you are prepared to fish sensibly for them. The right choice of bait is the real secret. I find that the majority of the large whiting I catch generally fall to whole sprat baits. Long strips of squid cut to resemble a sand-eel also produce good results, as do fish strip baits. Wherever possible, I try to avoid using soft baits for whiting, for I find that the fish tend to worry at the bait before actually taking it into their mouths. Their long sharp teeth will soon shred a soft bait, often reducing it to nothing without taking it properly.

Generally speaking, whiting feed just off the actual sea bed. Therefore a light two- or three-hook paternoster rig (see Fig. 12) is probably the best kind of terminal tackle to use. A light running leger with a long trace between lead and hook can also be useful, particularly when the tide is running too fast to use the paternoster properly. Unlike cod, whiting often go 'on feed' during the slack-water period—and when fish are scarce, this is often the period which can be relied upon to save the day.

Whiting should be fished for with as light a set of tackle as can be comfortably used. I have a little Abu Fladden boat rod which I use a great deal for whiting fishing, mainly for the sport it gives when I hook two or three goodish fish at a time. Whiting will come well to artificial lures, and a string of baited

74

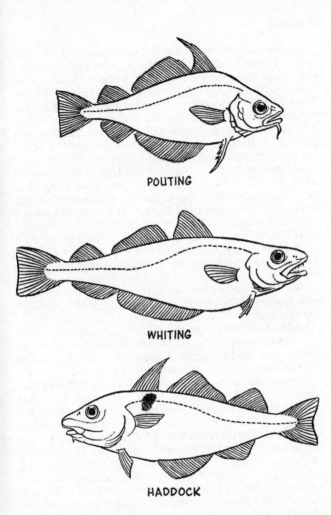

POUTING

WHITING

HADDOCK

mackerel feathers will often produce good catches. During the 1969 season I started to use small baited and unbaited pirk baits for catching whiting and found that the fish respond well to lures of this type.

Haddock

Very few anglers now have the opportunity to do much serious haddock fishing; for although these fish once had a widespread distribution, they have become rather rare in most localities due to being over-fished by commercial boats. To catch haddock in any quantity it is necessary to fish from the west coast of Scotland. Practically anywhere from the Isle of Arran up to Cape Wrath will produce haddock in vast numbers. Unfortunately, these Scottish fish tend to have a low average size, although the odd big fish can be taken.

In terms of quantity, my best haddock catches have all come from Loch Broom. On several occasions I have had over a hundredweight of fish in one day, fishing less than half a mile out from the jetty at Ullapool. The only other place I know that contains haddock in any numbers is the 'Field'— a mark directly out from the Dodman Point, several miles south of the fishing village of Mevagissey in Cornwall. Haddock of truly record-breaking proportions exist in this area and the average specimens weigh over 7 lb. At various times, I have done quite a lot of haddock fishing in this area and have been fortunate enough to boat a number of remarkably fine specimens.

Haddock are closely related to cod and there is a strong resemblance between the two species. The haddock, however can be easily identified by its slightly forked tail, black lateral line, and the dark spot on either side of its body.

Haddock are exclusively bottom feeders and, although they will eat small fish if they can catch them, their main food consists of marine worms, crustaceans, starfish and various molluscs. Standard whiting tackle is the best for haddock fishing, and most of the fish I have caught have been taken on fish or squid strip baits. A large haddock hooked on lightish tackle can put up a fair fight but, like the cod, it soon gives up.

During the winter of 1969–70, huge shoals of haddock appeared in the vicinity of the Thames Estuary and also at various points off the Essex coast. It is too early to say whether or not these shoals will take up residence in these areas—but if they do, they will provide excellent sport for local and visiting anglers alike.

Pouting

The only people, I am sure, who like to catch pouting are those anglers who specialise in salt-water competition fishing. To them, the greedy easily caught pouting must be a godsend. On most of the 'weigh ins' I have ever witnessed, 'pout' have been the main fish brought to the scales. Most ordinary anglers regard the pouting as little more than a bait-robbing nuisance; and even pouting of specimen size usually fail to arouse any enthusiasm in a normal boat-fishing party.

In appearance, the pouting is an attractive deep-bodied fish, copper in colour, with or without dark vertical stripes—depending on whether the fish lives on rocky or sandy ground. Pouting will take almost any bait and can be caught on any type of bottom-fishing tackle. Even very big pouting put up no resistance when hooked. Their flesh is rather tasteless when cooked, which is probably the main reason why few anglers are interested in catching them.

CHAPTER V

Sharks

FOUR species of shark provide sport for English boat anglers: the blue, the porbeagle, the thresher and the mako shark. The first three are the most common, but the mako is also present in British seas in reasonable numbers. Basically, it is the comparatively small blue shark that is most sought after. In the south-west of England, where these fish are prolific, a considerable number of shark boats specialising in blue shark fishing operate throughout the summer months. Similar boats also work off the west coast of Ireland where, again, blue shark are the main quarry.

The headquarters of the British Shark Fishing Club is at Looe, on the south coast of Cornwall, and Cornwall is still the premier shark-fishing area in the British Isles. Even as long ago as the latter half of the last century, sportsmen travelled to Cornish ports to fish for shark; and the post-war period has seen a boom in shark fishing.

Some years ago, when I worked a lobster-fishing boat on the grounds off the south-west side of the Isle of Wight, I often saw large porbeagle and thresher shark in the area between the Needles Lighthouse and St. Catherine's Point. This led to my writing an article on the possibility of catching big shark there. Soon after the article appeared in the *Angling Times*, two Fareham anglers made a determined effort to catch some of these fish—with the result that they not only brought a great many large porbeagle shark to the gaff in a short space of time but also broke the existing record for this species. That their record fish has since been beaten by an even bigger fish from the Channel Islands is immaterial. Their catches proved conclusively that big shark were present off the island in considerable numbers.

Since those initial successes, the Isle of Wight has been recognised as the best porbeagle and, to a lesser degree, thresher shark ground yet discovered anywhere around the British Isles. Now, shark fishing has become established in the area and many boats are available to anglers wishing to go out specifically to catch shark. More important still, the catching of quantities of large shark in a hitherto untried area started off a chain reaction in many other parts of southern England, with the result that fresh shark grounds were discovered and opened up by keen local anglers. At Bideford, for example, when shark fishing was tried for the first time some huge daily catches of small- to medium-sized porbeagles were taken; and similar reports came in from other areas as well.

It would seem likely that shark can be caught at almost any point in the English Channel, as well as in the Atlantic and the Bristol Channel. Whether or not they can be taken farther north of a hypothetical line drawn from the Wash across to Wales, no one as yet knows. Personally, I feel it very likely. Norwegian commercial fishermen work surface long lines well north of the Scottish islands, and some huge catches are made. So it would seem that it may well be possible to catch shark on rod and line from northern waters.

The general movement and habits of the four types of shark are detailed below.

Blue Shark

The blue shark is a streamlined fish which gets its name from its distinctive dark blue back and light blue sides. Unfortunately, these beautiful colours fade considerably as soon as the fish dies.

Blue shark weighing over 200 lb. have been caught in Cornish waters, and there is evidence to show that these fish can exceed a weight of over 300 lb. In warmer climates they grow to a huge size, but I would doubt that fish much over 300 lb. will ever occur off our coasts. The average size of rod-

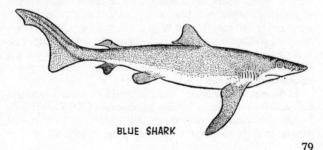

BLUE SHARK

caught blues is probably less than 60 lb., for a great many fish in the 40 lb. class are caught and destroyed each season. The minimum qualifying weight for membership of the Shark Club of Great Britain is 75 lb., and any fish of over 100 lb. can justifiably be regarded as a good catch.

Off Cornwall, catches of up to 28 blue shark have been made in a single day; and from large catches which I have helped to boat, it would seem that once feeding shark are located they are easy to catch in quantity.

Quite frankly, I do not think that any experienced shark fisherman regards the average run of blue shark as a sporting proposition. On standard shark-fishing tackle the majority of the fish caught put up little or no fight and can be played out and gaffed in a remarkably short space of time. In the West Country, the bulk of the shark caught fall to novice holiday-makers who, in all probability, have never fished before or since. Naturally enough, these people are apt to prolong the fight as they fumble with unfamiliar tackle and thrill to the pull of a large fish which, to them, is a dangerous man-eater of uncertain temperament. The knowledgeable angler, however, usually goes out blue sharking with a set of fairly light tackle in an effort to get some reasonable sport from any fish he hooks.

Blue shark being the commonest, they make a good starting species from whom the would-be shark fishermen can learn the basic techniques of sharking. Blues arrive off Cornwall at about the end of May and stay until the late autumn.

Porbeagle Shark

Apart from the odd porbeagle caught by anglers fishing from Cornish boats, little was known about the movements of porbeagle shark in British waters until the first big catches were made off the Isle of Wight. Even now, several years later, we still know very little really about these fish—although it is certain that beagles weighing at least 500 lb. live off the British coasts. It is possible that much larger fish live as yet undetected in Britain's seas.

In August 1969 a friend and I hooked five shark in a single day while boat fishing 5 miles south-east of St. Catherine's Point. The smallest weighed exactly 100 lb., and I was fortunate enough to hook a porbeagle we estimated at over

400 lb. I was also unfortunate enough to lose it 15 minutes later when it dived under the drifting boat, where it snagged and smashed my 80-lb. b.s. braided Terylene line.

Unlike blue shark, which tend to swim and feed well away from the land, porbeagles have a tendency to come in close to the shore in search of food. In my book *Rock Fishing* (Jenkins, 1969) I wrote about the possibility of catching these fish from the shore. The boat angler wishing to try his luck would be well advised to keep fairly close to the coastline at all times. I have seen big porbeagle shark basking in less than 40 ft. of water; and some of the most productive grounds off the Isle of Wight are not much deeper than this—proving conclusively that deep water is by no means their natural habitat.

I have noticed many times that this particular species of shark is attracted by strong tides and overspill areas. The dangerous tide-race off St. Catherine's Point is probably the main reason why big shark congregate in this area.

As a sporting species, the porbeagle has much to offer the angler. Its thick, muscular body and long fins give it a powerful outward appearance. Any angler lucky enough to make contact with a specimen weighing upwards of 100 lb. will soon realise just how much strength and endurance a big porbeagle can muster. There can be no comparison between this fish and the blue shark, for a porbeagle in good condition is a true game fish capable of providing even an expert angler with some truly thrilling fishing.

Thresher Shark

There can be no mistaking the distinctive outline of the thresher shark. The upper lobe of its tail is almost as long as its body, giving it a rakish overall appearance. Thresher shark are far more common than is generally supposed, although they are seldom hooked by the sport fisherman. No one can say for certain just how prolific this species is around the British Isles, for by nature the thresher is almost exclusively a bottom feeder which only appears on the surface when the summer mackerel are shoaling thickly.

This shark gets its name from the way it is alleged to use its great scythe-like tail to thresh the water in an attempt to round up small shoals of fish. I have certainly watched seven

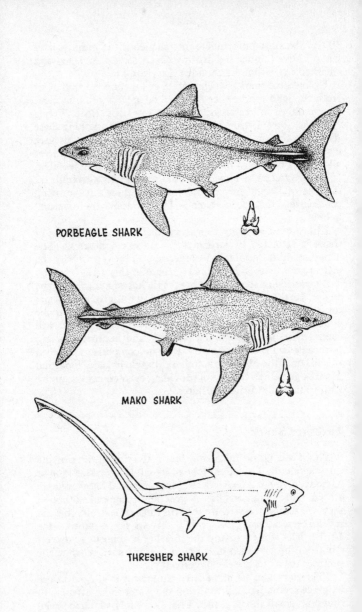

PORBEAGLE SHARK

MAKO SHARK

THRESHER SHARK

individual thresher shark rampaging about, whipping the water up into foam—but whether they were actually trying to group their prey I cannot truthfully say.

From the rod-and-line point of view, the thresher would appear to be a game and gallant opponent. I base this view not on personal experience but on seeing quite a good one caught by a fishing companion some years ago. Probably the main reason why few thresher shark are caught by anglers is that no one actually goes out deliberately to fish for them. The odd ones that are hooked usually fall to conventional off-the-bottom shark-fishing techniques. I am certain, however, that true bottom fishing is the only really practical way to catch these fish regularly.

I often hear of tope anglers hooking immense and totally unstoppable fish said to be monster tope but in all probability medium-sized threshers. Thresher shark to just under 300 lb. have been caught on rod and line, but it would seem likely that these shark can reach a weight of at least 500 lb. in British waters.

Mako Shark

This is the true aristocrat of the shark tribe—a handsome streamlined nomadic fish which is highly sought-after the world over by most true game fishermen. Mako shark have been caught for many years in the English Channel and mistakenly identified as porbeagle. In 1956, however, the teeth from a supposed record porbeagle were sent to the headquarters of the International Game Fish Association in New York, where they were positively identified as mako teeth.

Mako shark reach a weight of well over 500 lb. in British waters, and fish of double this weight are also thought to exist off the Cornish coast. Mevagissey, in south Cornwall, was at one time the premier mako shark port; but in recent years Falmouth has become the top mako town on the south Cornish seaboard.

I would doubt very much whether any mako shark yet caught in this country has been taken deliberately, for all those I have seen, caught or heard about have fallen to blue shark baits and tackle. I once hooked a good mako while drifting several miles out beyond the Eddystone Lighthouse, off Looe. This fish, like most mako shark, went away with a rush and jumped clean out of the water as I set the hook. Although not a monster, it did weigh over 200 lb., and, true to type, fought hard and long for every inch of line I gained.

At the time of writing, the only mako shark caught in Britain have all come from the West Country shark ports. But these fish are known nomads which can, and no doubt in due course will, turn up elsewhere. I am quite certain that sooner or later a mako will come from the Isle of Wight shark grounds—for where porbeagles go, so too will go the mako.

SHARK TACKLE

Rods

It is customary for most West Country shark boats to carry a selection of made-up rods which prospective customers can hire by the day. Unfortunately, most of this hire tackle is far too heavy to give the average run of shark the slightest sporting chance. Tackle manufacturers are also inclined to construct shark rods on the broom-handle principle—although there are now one or two firms which are producing well-designed rods specifically for shark fishing. As with most things, you get what you pay for. Although a good plain shark rod can be obtained for just under £10, a really superb rod will cost twice or three times as much.

Personally, I prefer solid glass shark rods. They are heavier than hollow glass, but I believe that they stand up better to the rigours of intensive shark fishing. Of the many solid glass shark rods I have tested, two stand out in my mind. One is the Sportex shark rod which retails at just under £10. The other is the Noris Shakespeare Boat Wonder, which costs just over £11. Both are very basic rods, but the Boat Wonder incorporates a full set of roller rings, whereas the Sportex has only a roller tip ring. Most of the more expensive shark rods incorporate either a full set of rollers, or a tip ring and a set of fully guarded lined rings which cut down wear and friction. Davenport & Fordham and Constable both make a series of rods matched to various line strengths. The heavier versions are ideal for all aspects of shark fishing but are expensive.

Always remember that a shark rod may well have to subdue a record fish. Failing this, it will undoubtedly catch many very large fish: so it pays to invest in the best rod you can afford. In general, the more you spend the better the quality of the rod and its furnishings.

Reels

Choice of reel for shark fishing depends entirely on individual taste. The majority of experienced shark men seem to prefer large capacity multiplier reels of the Penn Senator or Tatler type. I prefer to use a revolving drum reel and am fortunate enough to possess a pre-war Hardy Fortuna, complete with star drag and slipping reel drum. There are, of course, modern versions of this type of reel—the Allcocks Leviathan, for example, incorporates all the features of the old Fortuna. The Commodore reel, manufactured by the same company, is a simplified version of the Leviathan, having a brake lever instead of a star drag. The major disadvantage of a reel of this type is that when a fish runs out line the reel must revolve and, unless you can keep your hands clear of the spinning handle, bruised or cut fingers are a certainty. With the Leviathan or Fortuna type reel this cannot occur, for as the fish takes out line the drum itself revolves but the reel handle remains stationary. This applies also to the multiplier reels. My main reason for favouring the older type of reel is that its large drum has a terrific capacity which can only be equalled by the largest of multipliers. The cost of a good-quality shark reel ranges from £15 upwards, depending upon the size and make of reel required. Good second-hand shark-sized reels can often be obtained for a lot less than this. My Fortuna, for example, cost me only £5; and I recently purchased a practically new Tatler V, complete with 300 yards of 80-lb. Terylene line for only £12—a saving of well over £10.

Lines

Most shark are caught on float-fished baits. In consequence, it is best to use a line which has a natural buoyancy, ordinary nylon lines being of little practical use for shark fishing. Probably the best line to use is Dacron, which is made of braided polyester fibres. This is an imported American-made line. It is expensive but, being rot-proof, it will last for many seasons.

A cheaper but equally good line is the British-made Sea-ranger brand manufactured from braided Terylene. The beauty of braided line is that it will float and not stretch. Lack of elasticity is important, for it is very difficult to keep in contact with a big fish when the line continually stretches as pressure is applied to it.

85

The actual breaking strain of the line used depends entirely on the type and size of shark you expect to encounter. If, for example, blue shark are your main quarry, you could confidently use a line with a b.s. of 50 lb. If, on the other hand, porbeagles or threshers are known to exist in the area you intend to fish, then it would be safer to employ a heavier line.

Unfortunately, many anglers and boatmen take things to extremes and purchase line which is far too heavy for the job in hand. Lines of 120 lb. b.s. are commonly used on blue shark of a third of this weight, with the result that anything other than a truly enormous fish can be hauled in to the gaff within minutes of setting the hook. There is nothing very sporting about this sort of fishing: no matter how strong the fish is, it cannot hope to break the line—so the angler can apply as much brute force as possible to skull-drag the shark straight up to the boat.

The argument against using lighter lines is, of course, the possibility of hooking a real whopper of one type or another. If this happens, the angler simply has to take things easy. Instead of bullying the fish, he will have to settle down to a long and careful battle—which, after all, is the sporting part of shark fishing.

Where I do most of my shark fishing, porbeagles of well over 400 lb. are known to exist, and the average fish weigh from 150 lb. upwards. Because of this high average size, I habitually use a line with an 80 lb. b.s. Other anglers use heavier lines still, and from time to time we all get broken up by fish which we just cannot handle. But for everyday sharking, I find the 80-lb. line will do all I ask of it and still give the average shark a little leeway to show off its fighting spirit.

Hooks

For general shark fishing in Britain, a selection of hooks ranging from size 10-0 to size 16-0 should be carried. Mustads make the strongest hooks, and most up-to-date tackle shops keep a good supply of shark-size hooks in stock. Choice of hook size depends on two things: the size of the bait being used and the size of the shark expected to take it. Small blue shark, for example, can be caught on smallish mackerel or pilchard baits, so there is seldom any necessity to use a hook size larger than 10-0. For big porbeagle, thresher or mako sharks, however, a bait consisting of two large mackerel or a

4-lb. pollack or mullet would mask the point of a small hook, so a 12-14 or 16-0 hook should be employed.

Finally, a word of warning. Fish hooks of all sizes, particularly very large ones, are normally blunt when bought. Each should be carefully sharpened with a carborundum stone, both before and during use. This is vitally important. A large blunt hook is impossible to set in a shark's hard mouth.

Traces

Shark traces should always be made of wire. The sharp teeth of even a small shark will quickly cut through ordinary soft trace materials. Moreover, the rough hide of a shark will chafe through anything other than wire.

Shark traces can be bought from tackle shops or made up at home. Shop-bought ones are expensive, to say the least. To save money, my advice would be to make up your own terminal tackle. Nylon-covered braided wire can be bought by the yard from most tackle dealers. For sharking, it should have a b.s. of at least 120 lb. Many experts use even heavier wire than this, claiming—quite truthfully—that it is the trace that takes the most punishment during the fight.

Any shark-fishing trace should be at least 10 ft. long, for it must have enough length at all times to keep the actual line clear of the shark's rough skin. Single-length traces can be used, but most shark fishermen prefer to join two equal lengths of wire by means of a large barrel swivel. The addition of this swivel will help to eliminate the problem of the trace kinking, and therefore being weakened, during the time a good fish is being played out. Knots cannot be used with safety on any wire, and the only really practical way of attaching a hook or swivel to a heavy shark trace is to use a special brass crimp. Crimps can be purchased from tackle shops and come in a wide variety of internal diameters to suit different thicknesses of wire.

Crimping is simple. The wire passes through the crimp itself, through the eye of the hook or swivel, and then back through the crimp (see Fig. 24). A $\frac{1}{2}$-in. tail should be left, in case the crimp should slip slightly under strain. A special tool can be used for flattening out the crimp, but a pair of normal pliers will do the job equally as well. Crimps make a nice neat job and are the only practical way of joining hooks, etc., to heavy-duty nylon-covered wire.

A less expensive but highly effective shark trace can be

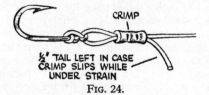

CRIMP

½" TAIL LEFT IN CASE
CRIMP SLIPS WHILE
UNDER STRAIN

Fig. 24.

made up from suitable lengths of Bowden bicycle-brake cable. This wire is strong, supple and easy to obtain. To join it, the wire should be passed through the hook or swivel, doubled back and lashed together with a short length of thin, soft, case wire (see Fig. 25). The whole join should then be soldered over, after which it should hold any shark that swims. This useful tip was passed on to me by a well-known Bournemouth angler Bob Bradshaw.

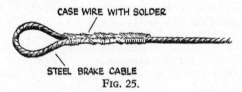

CASE WIRE WITH SOLDER

STEEL BRAKE CABLE

Fig. 25.

Shark Floats

Although it is possible to purchase ready-made floats large enough for shark fishing, the majority of shark anglers in this country much prefer to manufacture their own floats from any buoyant material that comes easily to hand. Empty plastic detergent or photographic developer bottles are the favourite. These need little adaptation to turn them into perfectly serviceable floats which have the added advantage of being virtually unbreakable.

The simplest way to turn one of these round containers into a sliding float is to tie a short length of old line tightly round the neck of the bottle, then attach a single swivel to the loose end of the line (see Fig. 26). The reel line can then be threaded through the open eye of the swivel and attached to the trace. The bottle-float is then free to slide up the line. A rubber stop can then be added at whatever distance one intends to fish, and the tackle is set to go.

Two crab-pot corks lashed together can also be used to support a shark bait, as too can a partially inflated balloon.

88

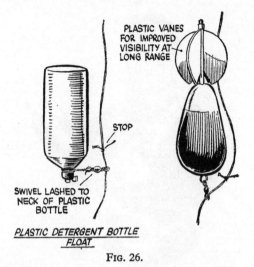

PLASTIC VANES FOR IMPROVED VISIBILITY AT LONG RANGE

STOP

SWIVEL LASHED TO NECK OF PLASTIC BOTTLE

PLASTIC DETERGENT BOTTLE FLOAT

FIG. 26.

Balloons, in fact, make very good shark floats which can either be tied directly to the reel line or attached by means of a swivel. The shape of the balloon is immaterial; but it is essential not to inflate it too much, otherwise a taking shark may well feel the drag of the over-buoyant balloon and drop the bait.

Gaffs

Every charter boat engaged in shark fishing carries a selection of large sharp gaffs. The individual boat owner who hopes to try his luck with the occasional shark-fishing trip will be well advised to follow suit. Three very big gaffs are essential; and all should be attached to the boat by a two-fathom rope, so that if a gaffed fish does tear the gaff out of your hands it will still be tied to the boat and can be hauled in again without undue trouble.

Sundry Items

A butt socket and shoulder harness (see Fig. 27) are advisable for catching big shark as they alleviate much of the strain and discomfort of trying to play a really big fish on a plain rod.

Bare trace wire can badly lacerate hands; so when grasping a long trace before gaffing a shark, always wear a pair of leather

89

BUTT SOCKET AND
SHOULDER HARNESS

FIG. 27.

gauntlets. My own are of the industrial type, which completely protect my hands from injury.

A large and lively shark can be very dangerous and difficult to handle once it has been brought inboard. Because of this, most professional skippers carry a 'priest' in the shape of a hammer, mallet or length of lead pipe. A couple of heavy blows on the tip of a shark's snout will often kill the fish immediately.

HOW TO HOOK SHARK BAITS

Every experienced shark angler has his own way of hooking and presenting his baits. Some carefully remove a portion of the backbone, then thread the hook through the bait in such a way that the hook point and barb project from the back of the fish (see Fig. 28). A simpler method, and the one which I prefer, is to pass the hook right through the tail section of the bait so that it hangs head down from the bend of the hook

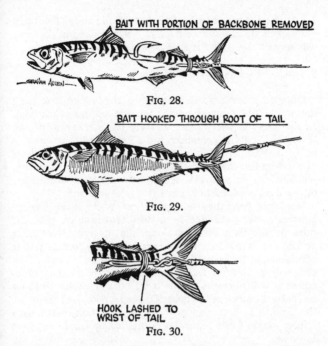

BAIT WITH PORTION OF BACKBONE REMOVED

Fig. 28.

BAIT HOOKED THROUGH ROOT OF TAIL

Fig. 29.

HOOK LASHED TO
WRIST OF TAIL

Fig. 30.

(see Fig. 29). To make sure it stays firmly in place, the wrist of the bait's tail can be lashed to the shank of the hook (Fig. 30). Two whole fish baits can be mounted one above the other (see Fig. 31).

Alternatively, the bait or baits can be hooked just once through the eye sockets and left hanging from the bend of the hook. This last method leaves the actual flesh of the bait totally unbroken—an advantage in rough water, which

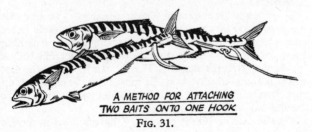

A METHOD FOR ATTACHING
TWO BAITS ONTO ONE HOOK

Fig. 31.

91

quickly breaks up a bait hooked through the body. The bony eye sockets do not tear easily, and a bait hooked in this way will stay on the hook for an indefinite period.

SHARK-FISHING METHODS

Once the shark grounds are reached, the first job is to hang the rubby-dubby container over the side or stern of the boat. In the West Country most sharkers use a wickerwork fish basket as a 'rubby' container, but a large-mesh bag can also be used. Basically, rubby-dubby is a smelly, oily mess of mashed-up fish-flesh and offal. Stale mackerel are a favourite, but herrings or pilchards are equally effective. Sometimes pilchard oil is added to the rather unpleasant mess.

Very few fishermen anchor a boat while shark fishing. Normally, the technique is to drift broadside-on with the tide. As the boat wallows along, the movement of water against the rubby-dubby container will keep a continual flow of fish oil and flesh particles washing away from the boat. This slick will trail out for several miles, and any shark that comes across it will normally follow it up until it comes within a catchable distance of the boat. To keep a good slick going all the time, it is necessary to pay strict attention to the container, adding fresh quantities of mashed-up fish at frequent intervals.

Once a satisfactory bait trail can be seen streaming away from the boat, the tackle should be baited and put over the side. Under no circumstances should more than three or, at the most, four rods be used at any one time—otherwise a hooked fish may collect other lines as it runs out, and the resulting tangle could take hours to sort out. Worse still, two or even three shark might be hooked simultaneously. I have seen this happen several times, and on each occasion all fish have been lost.

Shark are liable to feed at almost any depth. To find out just how deep they are on a given day, it is advisable to set each bait at different depths. For example, a boat fishing three rods should set the distance between float and bait at 20, 40 and 60 ft. respectively. The rig which catches the first fish will automatically show the most likely taking depth on that particular day, and the other tackles can be changed to correspond with the successful one.

On the Isle of Wight grounds, I have known porbeagle

shark to feed practically on the bottom; but most shark, other than the thresher, usually swim and feed fairly near to the surface. On hot calm days, particularly during periods of fine settled weather, shark tend to stay near the surface at all times and the tackle can be set accordingly at, say, 15, 25 and 35 ft. When the weather is rough and the water colder, however, it is baits fished well down towards the sea bed that are most likely to produce fish.

FISHING AT ANCHOR

Although, as yet, no one knows much about the movement and feeding habits of thresher shark, it is fairly certain that under normal circumstances they are a bottom-feeding species. In view of this, it would probably be better to choose a likely mark and anchor on it rather than fish for them on the drift in conventional shark-fishing style. The only thresher I have seen being caught was taken in this way on normal shark-weight gear, but with a running leger as opposed to the standard float-fishing rig used for other types of shark. Large threshers have, of course, been taken from time to time on float tackle, but never in any quantity. Just the odd fish here and there. This bottom-fishing idea is only a theory; but until someone discovers another way of taking thresher shark, this is the way I intend to fish for them.

SHARK FISHING AT NIGHT

In tropical waters, the vast majority of commercial shark fishermen operate at night. In this country no sport fisherman has, to the best of my knowledge, tried seriously to catch shark during the hours of darkness. I did try it once myself off the coast of Cornwall, and I hooked and lost a huge shark which jumped out of the water twice before shaking the hook free. I think, in fact, that night fishing for shark has tremendous potential. But to be successful, each trip would have to be planned very carefully; and two boats should fish the same grounds and keep in direct radio contact with each other at all times so that one could render assistance to the other in the event of emergency. I am sure that, in time, night fishing for shark will become a well-established practice in Britain and many new techniques will no doubt be developed especially for this style of angling.

HOW TO DEAL WITH A SHARK

Whenever a shark bait is in the water, the drag of the reel should be off so that a fish which takes the bait can run out the line without any check to its movements. It is strange how easy it is to forget to do this. More than one set of shark tackle has disappeared for ever simply because a check has been left engaged.

Far too many anglers are content to leave a shark rod to fish for itself while they eat, smoke, chat or sleep. This is wrong. Although it is not necessary or practical to sit holding the rod at all times, the float should be kept under constant observation so that, the moment a fish takes the bait, loose line can be pulled off the reel to give the fish a chance to take the bait decisively—for shark, contrary to popular belief, do not simply rush up and swallow the bait in savage fashion. Very often, quite the reverse applies. I have had bites from big porbeagles which have hardly caused the float to move at all, and yet I have hooked the fish well inside the mouth on the strike.

As with most fish, shark bites normally follow a definite pattern. First the float will bob down several times as the fish mouths at the bait. If it is satisfied that there is no danger, the fish will then move off, usually fairly slowly and gathering speed as it goes. This is the critical time. At the first sign of drag, the fish will open its mouth and eject the bait. Provided that the angler has seen the preliminary movements, however, and is holding the rod and feeding out loose line as the shark moves off, the fish can usually be relied upon to swallow the bait with confidence.

The first run of a big shark is very exciting, and it takes a cool head to keep calm as the loose line trickles steadily out through the rod rings. Judging the exact moment takes experience, but shark will very often slow up as they begin to swallow the bait. If they do not, then it will be necessary to strike as the fish is running off at speed. This can be a chancy business. Probably more shark are lost on the strike than at any other time.

The fight of a hooked shark varies considerably. One fish will give up without the slightest struggle; another will fight long and hard and test the tackle to its limit. When drifting for shark, the boatman must always be prepared to start the motor and chase the fish. This is particularly true of large mako or porbeagle which, left to their own devices, would soon run out every inch of line on the reel. Even so, it does not pay to keep too close to a well-hooked fish, for the drag imposed by a hundred yards or more of heavy braided line will help to wear out even a very big fish in a fairly short period of time. Normally, most hooked shark try to put as much distance between themselves and the boat as possible; but in August 1969, I hooked a brute of a shark on the Isle of Wight grounds which simply hung around the boat and totally ignored the constant pressure of the heavy tackle. Even while I played this fish, a second one estimated at over 200 lb. was nuzzling the rubby-dubby container right under my rod tip. Finally, at the end of 15 minutes hard work, the fish circled the boat about 40 ft below the surface and then made off under the boat, gradually rising to the surface as it ran. The result was that the line finally fouled the boat's keel and parted—and at no time was there anything I could do to stop this happening. I have never hooked a shark as powerful as this anywhere else round the British Isles and can only presume it to be a really huge specimen. We had other good fish that day, but nothing that fought as hard or as long as the lost fish. A big shark should be tied up tail first over the side of the boat (see Fig. 32).

SHARK ON ARTIFICIAL BAITS

Although I have never hooked blue, thresher or mako shark on artificial baits, I have had several porbeagle snatch at mackerel feathers. There can be little doubt that, as a species, porbeagles are inquisitive fish which I am sure would strike at large artificial baits. During the 1969 season, I watched a porbeagle weighing 100 lb. attack a blue balloon which was being used as a float. When the balloon burst, the fish simply went straight down and took the bait—hence the fact that I know its exact weight. On other days, I watched similar or larger specimens idly basking round the boat, nosing at any floating object that came their way. A mackerel or herring bait thrown directly at them was invariably taken with a rush and I am certain that a very big spoon-, plug- or fly-type lure would have been taken in the same way. I intend to try a shark-sized lure at the very next opportunity.

METHOD OF LASHING SHARK TO BOAT SO THAT SHARK HANGS HEAD DOWN

Fig. 32.

SHARK MARKS

I do not honestly believe there is any such thing as a shark mark in the accepted sense of the word, but there are areas in which shark tend to congregate. These places are what I call pack marks and—provided that such an area can be accurately pinpointed—sport can almost be assured. In my own area, the best shark grounds are usually fairly close to an overspill or tide race, round which the shark obviously gather to take advantage of the shoals of mackerel or other bait-sized fish which infest this kind of area. All shark are nomadic but they will hang around a place that can provide them with a plentiful supply of easy food.

In the open sea, shark often travel singly or, at best, in small groups; but close to a rich feeding ground they often group into large packs. Once a hotspot can be found, it will usually fish well for a whole season. This applies more to porbeagle than any other species, although on several occasions I have encountered a large concentration of blue shark. In one instance, two of us caught over 20 medium-sized blue shark in a single day—living proof that these fish also occasionally form into packs.

WINTER SHARK FISHING

There is some evidence to show that it may well be possible to catch shark out of the normally recognised season. Despite the general belief that all shark migrate to warmer climes with the onset of winter, commercial fishermen often encounter big shark while winter fishing for mackerel, herring or pilchard around the coasts of Cornwall. Winter shark fishing may, then, be a distinct possibility. Only time can show whether or not these fish remain behind in sufficient numbers to make them a worthwhile proposition for the winter boat angler.

CHAPTER VI

Conger and Ling

AFTER a lapse of almost 40 years, the conger record was recently broken twice in the space of two short weeks and as most knowledgeable anglers predicted, the new record fish tipping the scales at a massive 93 lb. came from one of the many wrecks off the south Devon coastline. This fish came as a direct result of a good boatman making an intensive and constructive attack on the monstrous eels known to inhabit the wrecks in this area. Since then the record has again been broken with a conger weighing 109 lb. 6 oz., and no doubt the next few years will see another record-breaker. The 120-lb.-plus conger can now be regarded as a definite possibility and the man who takes it will be a man who habitually employs extra heavy gear, for offshore wrecks contain many monsters that are more than capable of destroying all but the strongest of tackle. Conger of all sizes are furtive fish which idle away most of their lives by lurking under some type of obstruction. Wrecks afford them permanent homes, and a big conger firmly ensconced under a mass of jumbled metalwork can be an impossible object to budge.

Frankly, I believe that the luck element plays a bigger part in conger fishing than in any other aspect of angling. If you have the luck to hook a really big conger outside of its retreat, and if you have the luck to lift it up and away from its home in the first few seconds of the battle, then you will stand a fair chance of bringing it to the gaff. That is the kind of luck I mean.

Hooking conger is never a great problem; boating them,

CONGER

however, is an entirely different matter. Skill plays little part in the actual playing of a really large conger. The absolute novice with luck on his side is just as likely to break the record as the expert, if he can muster enough initial brute strength to pump the eel up and away from the sea bed.

Experience can, of course, be a great help but is, in my opinion, in no way essential. As a charter-boat skipper, I once took out an angler who, only a week before, had successfully caught a 72-lb. eel from a south Devon wreck mark. He told me at the time that this was the first conger he had ever caught and, prior to its capture, his best sea fish had been a 3-lb. pollack—a perfect example of the luck element playing a vital part in the successful killing of a very large conger eel. Nevertheless, it would be stupid to believe that all large conger are caught in this fashion. The vast majority of anglers who consistently boat large catches of big eels are very experienced indeed.

No one can really say just what weight conger can reach. There is much evidence to show that 200-lb. specimens are a possibility, although I doubt very much whether a fish of this calibre could ever be successfully caught on rod and line— for although it is basically a timid creature which retreats at the slightest sign of danger, a big conger is probably the most powerful and dangerous fish any sea angler can expect to encounter off British coasts. Even a heavy shark cannot stand comparison with a big conger for overall toughness. The power of a fighting conger is prodigious and it takes a strong, fit man to deal with a really large specimen.

Very big conger are normally regarded as an offshore species by most sea anglers, and deep-water wrecks are the places where most big conger are caught. The odd thing is, however, that the majority of the very large eels recorded have been found washed up in estuaries or on beaches. In several cases, the fish have still been alive when found; and in all instances I have traced, those that have been dead have been in a comparatively fresh condition—indicating, to my mind, that all of the fish had been living comparatively close to the shore and not well out to sea as most anglers suppose. A monster eel weighing 180 lb. was, for example, washed ashore on the French coast in 1961. Another of 142 lb. turned up on Walcott Beach, Norfolk, in 1956; and one weighing 96 lb. was found still barely alive at Minehead in Somerset in 1959. Two other specimens over the present record have also been found: one of 90 lb. washed up at Portland in 1956, and one weighing 86 lb. in the Orwell Estuary, Suffolk, in 1961. Finally, an eel weighing 84 lb. was washed ashore on the north Yorkshire coast in 1957, and an 87-lb. specimen was caught by hand on the North Wales coast in 1959. This last fish was left behind by the retreating tide and was said to be very much alive at the time it was found.

So with six fish equal to or well over the British record as material proof of the existence of very big conger in inshore waters, I would strongly advise keen conger fishermen to thoroughly survey likely marks close to the shore before pinning their hopes on distant deep-water grounds. I feel that many monster conger—some of record-breaking proportions —do live in areas where no one suspects their presence until they eventually die of old age or become too feeble to feed themselves properly and drift ashore, either as fresh corpses or in a severely weakened condition.

Conger legends are common, and every harbour, pier or estuary has its local versions. Many of these legends can be taken with a large pinch of the proverbial salt and dismissed as pure fantasy; but some of the stories are without the slightest shadow of doubt, based on absolute truth. In his book *A Tide of Fish*, Clive Gammon wrote of one such monster known as 'the Warrior' that lived around a wreck in Milford Haven, and I can think of half a dozen other marks which I have fished where I am fairly certain that conger of record-breaking size exist within a stone's throw of the shore. There are, for example, massive conger in the estuary of the Fowey River in Cornwall. Fish of similar size once existed around and just off the lighthouse quay at Mevagissey, again in Cornwall. Monster conger also live in the mouth of the Tamar River, in the Plymouth area.

Several of the old harbour walls on the west coast of Ireland shelter eels of unbelievable size. And what of Scotland? No one has written about conger fishing in Scottish waters, but there are plenty of conger there—and some pretty huge ones among them. A 101-lb. eel was caught in a prawn trawl off St. Abbs' Head, Berwick, in 1965—a fair example of how large conger can grow in Scottish waters.

Over the past 14 years, I have made a fair study of big conger in inshore waters and have reached the conclusion that they will live and grow to record-breaking size in comparatively shallow inshore areas if the area in question provides them with shelter and a regular supply of food. Mevagissey Harbour, for example, once contained conger of great size which lived in various holes along the outer quay wall. These fish were assured of a regular supply of food, for not only did the long-line boats dump all their unused bait into the harbour after each trip but also the entrails from their catches and the offal from the pilchard cannery in the town were dumped twice daily from the outer side of the sea wall. The resident conger therefore got the maximum amount of food with the absolute minimum amount of effort, with the result that they had a remarkably fast growth rate. I have had conger to nearly 50 lb. while shore-fishing this area and have been present when conger of over 70 lb. have been caught from boats anchored less than 100 yards from the quay wall.

Unfortunately, the decline in the Cornish fishing industry during the late 1950s and early 1960s put paid to the conger fishing at Mevagissey. When most of the fish stores, and the pilchard-canning factory closed down, the congers' main food supply abruptly ceased. About the same time, the quay foundations were inspected and the holes which the conger used for shelter were blocked in. Sub-aqua divers who carried out the preliminary inspection on the quay stonework assured me that each large hole had its resident conger, some of which were estimated to weigh over 100 lb. This I can believe, for on several occasions I hooked and lost conger of immense size while fishing in the quay area. One huge fish even smashed a special double-built split-cane rod and twisted the seat of my large diameter centre-pin reel in a straight run. Despite the fact that the rod parted and the reel buckled, the line held—although I was powerless to stop the fish from slithering under some immovable obstruction and I was finally forced to break the line by hand. I quote this particular story to illustrate the kind of situation that can occur when conger in inshore water have plenty of cover and a consistent supply of food literally dumped on their doorstep. This condition occurs in hundreds of fishing harbours all around the British Isles.

The Scottish fishing harbours where commercial fishing is still very much alive are an obvious place to expect to find big conger close inshore. An example of this is Lochalsh—the ferry point between the mainland and the Isle of Skye. Herring drifters unloading fish at this village consistently dump huge weights of fresh mackerel into the sea off the quay wall, and even in broad daylight I have seen hefty conger taking advantage of the free meals the drifters provide. Local inshore fishermen have assured me that conger of huge proportions live within a few hundred yards of this quay.

101

Judging by the many similar ports all round the Highlands and the islands, the whole aspect of conger fishing in Scottish waters is well worth serious consideration. At present, sea anglers are on the verge of a new frontier. No doubt the next decade will produce some startling results—particularly with large fish like conger, which are now becoming increasingly popular with boat anglers.

I said earlier in this chapter that conger to at least 200 lb. are known to exist. The 180-lb. specimen already mentioned was only 20 lb. under this fantastic weight: but even this monster is small in comparison to the 250-lb. brute caught in a trawl net by a Belgian fishing boat operating off the Westmann Islands. This incredible eel, like the others mentioned, was caught in recent times, being trawled in 1962—proof, indeed, that eels of nearly three times the present record weight still exist.

Conger have a wide distribution, but, generally speaking, they are commonest off Britain's south and south-west coasts. Normally, they live in rocky areas or artificially created retreats like large wrecks. Although they are in no way a shoaling species, they are gregarious. Large numbers of eels of all sizes will live in close proximity to one another in apparent harmony. The females grow to a much greater size than the males. There is, in fact, a widespread belief that the outsize specimens are usually barren females which, being unable to spawn, feed continuously right up until the time they die. All the very big fish found either dead or dying appear to have been in reasonable condition, which would indicate that death strikes mature eels very rapidly.

Conger can be caught at almost any time of the year, but the late summer and autumn months usually fish the best. In the West Country, long-line boats catch fantastic numbers of large conger at this time of the year, very often from inshore waters. One friend of mine working a 22-ft. boat out of Mevagissey had a 170-stone catch of large conger in a single day. This included a number of fish weighing between 60 and 80 lb. The entire catch was taken less than a mile out from a mark inside the Gwineas Rock.

It is a popular fallacy that conger are 'dirty' feeders which live for the most part on rotten fish gleaned from the sea bed. This is nonsense. As a general rule, conger are much less inclined to eat stale food than, say, skate or ray. I have caught the odd conger on a stinking bait, but have always found stale baits to be definitely inferior to fresh ones when conger are the quarry. So take my advice and use the freshest bait you can get. In this way, you will catch plenty of conger.

TACKLE

In my opinion, it is totally impossible to over-estimate the strength of a very large conger. Far too many anglers make the mistake of seriously under-estimating the terrific power of these great eels. There is nothing on the British fish list more capable of showing up a weakness or defect in tackle than an enraged conger, yet anglers still persist in going to sea with what they consider to be sporting tackle. My advice is to forget any preconceived idea that conger are a sporting species which should be given a fair opportunity to show off their paces. Such a foolish idea is probably one of the main reasons why the conger record has stood for so many years.

Under no circumstances can light or medium gear be used for hunting big conger. They fight in a completely different way from all other fish, making it impossible to play them in a conventional fashion. Sheer brute force is the only tactic likely to beat a big conger—and it's brute force from both ends, at that. So do not make the mistake of hooking a possible record-breaker on tackle that cannot stand constant punishment, otherwise you too will join the ranks of the many, many anglers who have made that mistake and lived to regret it.

Choice of tackle depends on two things: where you intend to fish, and the size of the conger you may possibly hook. For wreck fishing, I use shark gear and would recommend a heavy solid or hollow glass shark-type rod, matched with a large capacity multiplier or centre-pin reel holding a minimum of 300 yards of 60- to 80-lb. b.s. braided line. Eighty-pound line may sound ridiculously strong, but it is not over-heavy when it comes to forcing a big eel out from under some solid underwater obstruction. Even a thirty-pounder with its broad, flat tail firmly wrapped round a snag can test this sort of tackle to the utmost, and a hundred-pounder could exert enough brute strength to snap a line like this without too much trouble if it had a firm grip with its tail around something substantial. For less snaggy areas, where the average fish weighs between 15 and 30 lb., a lighter set of tackle can be used. Off the Isle of Wight, for example, where

103

conger of over 40 lb. are by no means common, most keen conger men use a medium-weight boat fishing outfit and 40-lb. b.s. line. Each season, however, the odd outsized eel is encountered in these waters and—with the exception of a near-60 lb.-specimen which was hooked well away from the nearest immovable snag—the result is invariably the same: a broken line, and sometimes even a smashed rod—a lasting reminder that large conger should not be hooked on anything other than the strongest of tackle.

I remember once taking a night charter party out to a productive conger mark in Scratchells Bay, near the Needles, Isle of Wight. In all, we caught 18 conger to 42 lb. and had three rods broken by exceptionally large eels. I lost count of how many times fish were lost through the lines breaking, but well over a dozen good fish were lost in this way; and the party had trouble with the fish they caught—and my own forty-two-pounder, although a good fighter, never once came close to breaking free. This, I think, was one of those rare occasions when the giants were hard on the feed: a time when all of us should have had tackle that was heavy enough to force the fish up from the sea bed.

My advice would be to always make a habit of fishing heavier than usual when after conger. Monster fish are by no means commonly encountered, but it is advisable to be fully prepared for the eventuality. There can be no question of being unfair to conger by using a line which has a breaking strain of twice the weight of the average fish. As I said earlier, fighting a conger of any reasonable size is a matter of brute strength rather than skill and the only tactics worth using are the ones that employ the rod line and reel as a lifting device rather than as a buffer against which the eel can exhaust its strength. A conger rarely attempts to run when it feels the hook, the only exception being on the rare occasion that it is hooked well away from its hole. Normally, however, the eel will be in or close to its retreat when it takes the bait. The moment the hook is set, the angler must be prepared to use the rod and reel like a crane and winch to lift the eel as far up off the sea bed as possible during the first few seconds of the battle. This is the really critical part of fighting a conger. Once it gets its head down, it has every chance of going firmly to ground and breaking the line. But if it can be lifted and pumped well up clear of the bottom, there is every chance that it will be successfully boated.

A conger hauled out of its natural habitat tends to fight in a way peculiar to itself. Instead of running, it will usually perform intricate figure-eight movements, jagging its big head about in a desperate attempt to loosen the hook. If this tactic fails, it will then start to spin—gradually increasing its speed as it nears the surface. Throughout all this, the rod and line are taking a terrific beating—an added reason for using extra-heavy gear at all times.

Terminal Tackle

A conger's jaw is lined with a mass of short, very sharp teeth. These, combined with the tremendous crushing power of the jaw, will quickly cut through a normal nylon trace. Nowadays, most conger men use braided nylon-covered wire as trace material. This is far superior to the heavy single-strand wire traces which many tackle shops still stock and sell as conger traces. Stiff wire of this kind should be avoided at all cost. Despite their ugly appearance and incredible strength, conger are surprisingly cautious and delicate feeders which are apt to drop a bait attached to a stiff length of heavy single-strand wire trace. The braided covered wire is, of course, flexible and far less likely to alarm a feeding fish.

A good conger trace should incorporate at least two swivels. These will help to eliminate the kinks a spinning eel can put into the trace as it fights for its life. Commercial fishermen who catch conger on special long lines normally employ a hook which has a built-in swivel device (see Fig. 33). This type of hook is too narrow in the gape for normal rod-and-

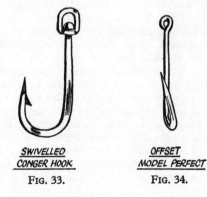

SWIVELLED
CONGER HOOK
FIG. 33.

OFFSET
MODEL PERFECT
FIG. 34.

line fishing. The hook I would advise every conger angler to use is the Allcocks stainless steel sea hook size 6-0 or 8-0. This hook is extremely strong and can be easily sharpened with a carborundum stone. It also has an offset point (see Fig. 34), which makes it ideal for bony-mouthed fish like conger. One of these hooks on a 3-ft. length of double-swivelled wire (see Fig. 35) is ideal for all forms of conger fishing. The wire should have a breaking strain equal to the b.s. of the actual reel line.

It pays to check the trace after each fish has been caught. The easiest way of ascertaining that the wire is undamaged is to run it through the fingers once or twice. At the slightest sign of roughness or even flatness on the outer sheath, the trace should be changed. Weak spots like this usually break under pressure.

SWIVELLED WIRE TRACE

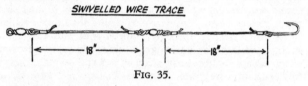

FIG. 35.

ANGLING METHODS

Legering is the best boat-fishing method to use for conger, and it is essential that the line should run easily through the lead link—for despite their large size and great strength, conger are wary fish and will eject a bait the moment they detect any additional drag on the line. Conger are, of course, true bottom feeders; so to be successful, the bait should rest right on the sea bed. Because of this, it is advisable to use a short trace between lead and hook. In fact, most experienced conger men allow the first trace swivel to act as a stop for the lead link. To avoid the possibility of this fouling up, I use a 2-in. length of aquarium-type polythene tube and two large plastic beads between the lead and the trace swivel (see Fig. 36). A normal conger trace is $2\frac{1}{2}$ ft. to 3 ft. long, which gives ample distance between lead and bait. Longer traces can be a drawback, for in a strong tide a long trace will allow a bait to lift up from the bottom. The line between rod tip and lead should be kept taut at all times. Conger are delicate feeders, and if there is any slack in the line many preliminary bites may go undetected.

106

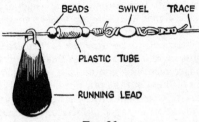

FIG. 36.

Because conger invariably live close to rocks or other solid obstructions, tackle losses during a conger session can be rather high. Most 'hang ups' occur when the lead rather than the reel line or wire trace becomes jammed in a crevice. To cut tackle loss to a minimum, it pays to attach the lead to a few inches of line of a lesser breaking strain than the actual reel line. In the north of England, this is known as 'rotten bottom tackle'. A swivel can be used as a sliding link (see Fig. 37) so that if the lead does become snagged up the weaker line will snap under rod pressure, leaving the reel line and trace intact. The swivel will, of course, also stay in position. A new lead can then be quickly fastened to it so that fishing can continue with the minimum amount of time wasted.

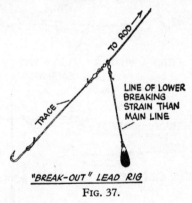

"BREAK-OUT" LEAD RIG

FIG. 37.

CONGER BAITS

The best conger bait is undoubtedly a large chunk of fresh squid or cuttlefish. Small, whole imported squid can also be used; but although deep frozen, they are seldom as effective as fresh baits. Some boat anglers believe that squid baits should be thoroughly pounded with a wooden mallet before use. Conger are said to be attracted to 'tenderised' baits of this type. But there is little truth in this theory. I still meet the odd conger man who continues to use squid baits prepared in this fashion, but the practice is definitely fading out.

Where fish baits are concerned, conger have very catholic appetites and almost any type of fish can be turned into bait, provided that it is fresh. Oily fleshed baits like mackerel, pilchard or herring are probably the best because conger appear to hunt by scent as much as by sight. An oil slick exuding from a bait will usually attract eels in the vicinity.

When very big conger are known to frequent a particular mark, it is advisable to use a large bait. Big conger, like most heavy fish, tend to be lazy and are more inclined to swallow one large offering rather than have to work hard at picking up a number of small baits. For conger of average size, one good mackerel should make three baits (see Fig. 38). A fillet bait

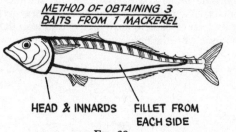

METHOD OF OBTAINING 3 BAITS FROM 1 MACKEREL

HEAD & INNARDS   FILLET FROM EACH SIDE

FIG. 38.

MACKEREL FILLET TIED TO LINE ABOVE HOOK

FIG. 39.

from the side of the fish should be lashed to the line, above the eye of the hook, with a length of darning wool or elastic thread (see Fig. 39) so that it does not slide down the hook shank and bunch up on the bend of the hook. A bait that is allowed to do this will rarely catch fish as well as one which has been properly presented.

When cutting fish baits for conger, great care should be taken to remove the head with the guts still attached. This is a deadly bait for conger, and for most other large bottom-feeding fish as well. The softness and the smell of the hanging guts is, without doubt, the main reason why this bait will catch fish when all others fail.

Whole small pouting, pollack, wrasse or flatfish make good conger baits. These can be used either alive or dead. Dead baits should be hooked through the wrist of the tail, and their side should be scored with a sharp thin-bladed knife (see Fig. 40). The cuts will allow the juice of the bait to trickle away to form a scent trail for the fish to follow. Live baits

KNIFE CUTS TO ALLOW JUICES TO ESCAPE

FIG. 40.

should be hooked through the upper lip so that they hold their position facing into the flow of water. A bait hooked in this fashion will remain alive and kicking for a considerable period of time. A live bait hooked through the root of the tail will quickly drown due to water pressure pushing back through its gills. Conger are active hunters and catch most of their food alive.

GROUNDBAIT

It has been proved conclusively that conger of all sizes are attracted by groundbait. In many areas it is common practice to fasten a mesh bag full of mashed-up fish to the anchor before throwing it over the side (see Fig. 41). The only draw-back to this is that when there is an extra-strong tide running, and there is a lot of rope between boat and anchor, the conger tend to become concentrated well in front of the angler's bait.

There are, of course, specially produced groundbait cubes manufactured from compressed and highly concentrated fish extract. These are sold complete with tiny mesh bags, which

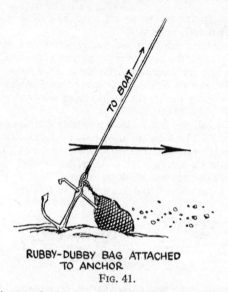

RUBBY-DUBBY BAG ATTACHED
TO ANCHOR

Fig. 41.

should be attached to the swivel that joins the trace and reel line. There can be no question that these cubes work. Unfortunately, however, on the grounds I fish, the conger make a habit of eating the groundbait complete with net bag in preference to the actual bait. I am sure that groundbait does help to attract conger and, as a general rule, would advise its use whenever conditions allow.

CONGER BITES

Conger of all sizes are inclined to play with a bait for some time before actually taking it into their mouths. Normally, the bigger the fish the gentler it will be with the bait. Very small conger tend to rattle the rod tip violently as they mouth at the bait.

Quite a lot of anglers lose conger by striking far too soon at a taking fish—without doubt, a reflex action. But where conger are concerned, patience is essential. Generally, the first indication that a conger has found the bait comes when the rod tip is pulled slowly down and then released. As soon as this initial movement is felt, the rod tip should be lowered to give the hungry fish a few inches of line to play with. At the same time, it is advisable to disengage the reel spool so that as the biting eel takes up the slack line it can take additional line freely. In this way, the fish can be induced to take the bait properly.

Conger never appear to be in much of a hurry with a bait. As much as ten minutes may elapse between the time the first bite indication is received and the time when the eel can be felt actually moving off and away with the bait. To avoid dragging the bait away from the eel, the strike must only be made when the fish actually begins to run out line. Providing one is prepared to relax and ignore the first twitchy bites, hooking a conger is a simple enough operation; but it is surprising just how many anglers are unable to control their striking reactions and lose their fish by pulling the bait away from it.

Strangely enough, although a conger which has had a bait dragged away from it can seldom be induced to feed again, one that has been lost after being played half way up to the boat will often go straight back down and snatch the remains of the bait. I have known a number of conger do this in the past and can only conclude that the fish becomes so annoyed at the way it has been handled that it is determined to kill and eat the apparent enemy at all cost.

HANDLING CONGER

How you handle and boat a hooked conger depends on the size and freeboard of the boat you are fishing from. On a large charter boat with plenty of deck space, the thrashing eel can be gaffed inboard and dropped either on to the deck or into a large fish container. Conger and shallow fish-boxes definitely do not go together: an eel will soon get its strong tail over the rim of the box and lever its body out on to the deck. Because of this, most charter boats are equipped with plastic dustbins which are deep enough to hold average eels without fear of them escaping. For small-boat work, however, there is not usually room for a bulky container of the dustbin type. Under such circumstances, it is best to drop the eel straight into a strong heavy-duty sack. The hook trace should be cut from the reel line so that the fish can be unhooked ashore, where one has plenty of space to work.

Under no circumstances should conger be allowed to lie loose in the bottom of a small boat. Their body-slime will

111

quickly turn the boat into a miniature ice rink, and there is always the chance that they might bite. In any case, a slip on a bait may well cause a fatal accident.

The sight of a writhing conger seems to stir many anglers to an excitement probably motivated by fear of the fish. Invariably, their first reaction is to grasp the nearest blunt instrument and try to kill the fish with it. This, again, can be dangerous—especially in dinghy-type boats. More than one angler has missed his target and stove in the bottom of his boat. This may appear to have its funny side: but it does happen more frequently than most people realise, and the results can be serious. Anglers have also been known to attempt to stick a sharp knife into a conger's brain. This can be very dangerous indeed, for a conger of any size is likely to twist its body, turning the knife in the process and severely cutting the hand that holds it.

My advice is to leave the conger alone as much as possible. Only remove the trace if the hook is in the lip of the fish, and never attempt to probe down an eel's throat in an attempt to extract tackle. 'Dead' eels have a nasty habit of suddenly coming to life—and the sharp, tooth-filled jaws of a reasonably large eel could amputate fingers.

It may seem that I am overstressing the dangers involved: but remember that an accident at sea is far more dangerous than one on land, for you are a long way from a hospital or help of any kind.

A strong gaff should be carried in the boat at all times.

THE EFFECTS OF WEATHER ON CONGER

The best time to catch conger on inshore grounds is on a very warm, dark night. Thundery evenings are quite good as well. If the sky is overcast, with little or no wind, good sport can be almost guaranteed. Inshore conger are almost exclusively nocturnal feeders, but over deep-water marks the fish can be expected to feed at all times of the day—presumably because light does not penetrate water beyond a certain depth.

Conger are usually uninclined to feed on cold, clear nights; and in shallow water, a sudden snap of frosty weather will often kill off most of the resident eels. During the exceptionally cold winter of 1962–3, the mortality rate of conger in inshore waters was exceptionally high. In many areas, huge numbers of conger perished during this period. Most of the very big conger that have been washed up in a dead or dying condition have been found during the winter months.

Ling

Although ling have elongated, eel-like bodies, they are actually members of the great cod family. They are easy to distinguish from conger on account of their long bodies, broad heads and wide, tooth-filled mouths. They have two dorsal fins, and a single long barbule under the chin. Varying considerably in shade from one locality to the next, they are usually a grey or greeny-brown colour. In some, the body is mottled with darker spots and blotches. The smaller fish seem more prone to this mottled effect, and in all probability the spots fade away as the fish reach maturity.

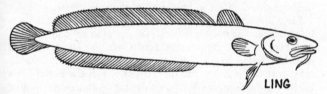

LING

Ling, like conger, can grow to a vast size. Specimens of over 70 lb. have been taken by commercial methods; but any angler fortunate enough to boat a ling of over 20 lb. can be justifiably proud of his catch, although ling in excess of 40 lb. have been taken on rod and line.

As a fighting species, ling are a better proposition than conger. Most of those I have caught have made several long runs before rolling up to the gaff. A twenty-eight-pounder which I hooked while fishing on a mark south-east of the Lizard Peninsula, Cornwall, fought extremely hard, for its size. I was convinced at the time that I had hooked a good-sized tope, for the ling's fast erratic runs were very similar to the standard fight-pattern of tope.

Ling, like conger, are lovers of wrecks and sunken rocks. Unlike conger, however, ling can sometimes be induced to feed well up off the bottom. Oddly enough, in Cornish waters I have often found very large ling over flat-bottomed marks where there is little or no cover. Presumably, the extra-big fish have a nomadic streak and will wander out over the sand in search of food. I have had several 20-lb.-plus specimens while drifting over sandy ground in this way. Probably the greatest ling catch ever made by British anglers was one of over 1,500 lb. of fish caught in deep water over the wreck of the *Lusitania*, out from the Old Head of Kinsale in southern Ireland. Well known sea-angling photographer Michael Barrington-Martin, who led this party, had fish up to 43½ lb. —truly magnificent fishing for a total catch which has yet to be equalled.

I have always found ling to be greedy fish. Once they can be induced to feed, sport can be assured. Unlike the conger, which tends to be a cautious feeder, a big ling is a voracious biter which will pull the rod tip hard down as it engulfs the bait. Ling are true predators and can be caught on all types of squid and fish bait. On the famous foghorn mark off Fowey, I have hooked some very good ling on live pouting baits. Around the Eddystone Reef, however, I have always found fresh mackerel fillets to be the most successful lure.

Ling are hard fighters, and robust tackle is essential for ling fishing. Light conger tackle is the kind of gear to use. Anything much lighter could easily lose you an exceptional fish. Big ling hooked close to some obstruction invariably make a dive for home the moment they feel the hook. This initial power-dive can be very difficult to stop—but stop it you must; for once the fish gets its head down into cover, a breakage is almost inevitable. Ling often make long runs against heavy rod pressure. Although they often do not fight as long as conger of similar size, they are more of a sport fish than the eel. Basically, conger-type terminal tackle should be used to catch them. But the length of trail between hook and lead should be increased by at least 2 ft., for ling are more active feeders than conger and seem to prefer a bait which moves about a bit with the flow of the tide.

I think that Scottish waters will produce some very big ling in future seasons. As yet, only a few Scottish sea-fishing grounds have been exploited, but some very good ling catches have been reported. These indicate high stocks of this species off the Scottish coasts which time and consistent fishing must prove to exist.

CHAPTER VII

Bass

BASS are unmistakable fish. Even anglers who have never actually seen one in the flesh before will have little trouble identifying the first specimen they catch. The bass belongs to the perch family and, like its freshwater cousin, has a large spiny dorsal fin. Its neat, extremely compact body is covered with hard, firmly attached scales, giving the fish a rugged yet streamlined appearance. Bass, particularly small ones, vary in colour from bluish-grey to greenish-grey on the back, with brilliant burnished silver flanks and white underparts. Very large bass sometimes have dusky grey backs and rather tarnished silver sides.

A bass in prime condition is a muscular, heavy-shouldered fish with a hard head and huge mouth, obviously well suited to a hard life in rough water. Most rod-caught bass range from 2 to 6 lb. A fish weighing over 10 lb. can be looked upon as a really outstanding specimen. The largest bass yet caught in Britain on rod and line tipped the scales at over 18 lb. Monsters of this calibre are, however, extremely rare, and they are becoming rarer with the passing of each successive season. Commercial fishermen occasionally take fish over the record size, and it would seem that under favourable circumstances bass can attain a weight in excess of 20 lb. Once, in a Portuguese fishing village, I saw the weighing of a monster bass which pulled the scale over to exactly 25 lb. I do not ever expect to see bass of this size caught in English waters.

Unfortunately, sea anglers are slow to realise the value of conservation. Bass—which are, at best, slow growing—are among the species which have become seriously depleted by over-fishing both on a sporting and a commercial basis. If there is to be any future for the bass, it is essential that the club anglers and individual anglers set themselves a limit and adhere to it at all times. One still reads of huge bags of prime fish being caught and killed from marks like the Udder Reef off Fowey, in Cornwall, the Eddystone Lighthouse, the Gwineas Rock, south Cornwall, etc., and invariably the anglers who make these vast hauls justify the mass destruction of invaluable breeding stock by stating that the fish they have caught are simply a drop in the ocean in comparison with the fantastic shoals that congregate on these prolific grounds. This may well be true; but a few years of such mammoth

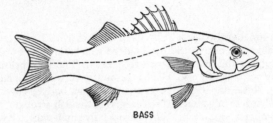

BASS

catches will destroy the big shoals for ever—and a once fine fishing area will be ruined for eternity.

The Splaugh Rock, off southern Ireland, is a typical example of the dangers of over-fishing a particular area. This mark, once one of the most famous bass grounds anywhere in the British Isles, now produces very little. The once huge bass shoals which were decimated almost daily are a thing of the past, and it is very doubtful whether they will ever return. The blame can be laid directly at the angler's door. Commercial fishermen are always being blamed for ruining good fishing grounds, but it is one thing to catch 500 lb. of big bass to sell on a commercial basis and another thing entirely to kill a similar quantity of fish on the pretext of sport. No angler can dispose of huge quantities of large bass privately: and if he sells them, then I am afraid he cannot class himself as a sporting fisherman. The Splaugh Rock is just one example of the outcome of constant over-fishing. But fortunately, the Irish fishery trusts have learned their lesson and are already imposing limits on the amount of bass which can be caught and killed in one day.

I suppose that, at some time or another in his career, every bass addict has been guilty of killing a large number of fish. I know I have. But as soon as I realised that I could not dispose of the majority of my catch, I acknowledged the stupidity of bringing home fish which I could not possibly hope to use or give away. So I promptly discontinued the practice. Now, I only retain fish for which I know I can find a use. This does not mean that I stop bass fishing the moment I have taken my self-imposed limit; but it does mean that I set myself a higher standard and immediately return every fish under that weight to the sea. Far too many anglers get a sort of blood lust when the fish are biting freely, and they kill everything they catch without a thought for sport in future seasons. Worse still, in my own area some anglers have discovered that small bass make first-class live bait, with the result that bass stocks are now being further depleted to supply baits for tope fishing. This is a practice which should be frowned upon by fishery authorities and club officials alike. In my opinion, anglers found guilty of using live or dead bass to catch tope or any other large predator should be expelled from their angling club or penalised by the Fishery Board. There are plenty of pouting, wrasse, etc., that can be used for bait without killing future bass stocks just because their silver sides attract tope.

Bass can be caught from the Suffolk coast round to the Welsh coast, becoming more and more common the farther south you go. It would seem, in fact, that bass possibly have a far wider distribution than most people realise. During the past season or so, quite a few have been taken from the west coast of Scotland—particularly in Luce Bay—and it would seem likely that consistent fishing in this and similar areas of the Scottish coastline could prove that bass frequent northern waters in far greater quantity than has been supposed. The south and north coasts of Devon and Cornwall provide wonderful bass fishing, as do marks on the west coast of Wales. In Irish waters, bass fishing is often superb.

In my own area, the marks around the Isle of Wight produce many very big bass—a boat fisherman live-baiting in Alum Bay, for example, caught a monster fish weighing 16¼ lb.—and the 'bridge' off the Needles Lighthouse is often thick with bass of all sizes. The Shingles, in Christchurch Bay, are often alive with very big bass, and the run at the mouth of Poole Harbour, in Dorset, can generally be relied upon to produce several double-figure specimens during each season. In the West Country, large estuaries are favourite venues with men who specialise in small-boat fishing for large bass. The Dart, Teign, Fowey, Exe, Tamar and Fal river estuaries are all first-class bass grounds, but I suppose the Fowey is the most famous West Country bass river.

Strangely enough, bass are attracted by fresh or brackish water and there have been many instances of individual fish, usually large ones, making long upriver journeys. On the Arun

117

River in Sussex many very big bass were once caught on dace livebaits intended primarily for pike.

Basically, bass are a rough water species which thrive in heavy seas and areas subjected to tide rips or overspills. Offshore rocks or reefs which cause the sea to churn and foam are ideal places to hunt for them, and the rougher the water the better the chance of catching good-sized fish. The Eddystone Reef is a typical example of an offshore bass mark. This reef, which can only really be fished in comparatively fine weather, will normally produce good bass catches at all times —and there are occasions when the sea around the rocks is black with fish. The Gwineas Rock, situated midway between Mevagissey and Gorran Haven in south Cornwall, is another offshore mark where bass sometimes congregate in incredible numbers. Oddly, when they shoal like this they can rarely be induced to feed. This can be most frustrating, particularly when the fish can be clearly seen in the water.

Although bass can be caught at practically any time of the year, the effective bass-fishing season lasts from the middle of April until early October. During very mild winters, bass in West Country waters may stay throughout the winter months as well; but as a rule, the first onset of wintry weather drives the fish out into deep water well away from the coasts. In my experience, the best bass-fishing months are May, June and September.

Very little is yet known about the spawning habits of bass although the Irish Inland Fishery Trust has been carrying out a great deal of research on the subject. The research has now been going on for four years, and I hope that it will result in a greater understanding of bass breeding habits which could, in turn, help anglers catch bigger and better fish. Tiny bass are often very common in estuarial waters, and I am therefore inclined to believe that bass spawn close to the shore; but as yet, I have no definite proof of this.

Bass in calm waters or estuaries often show their whereabouts by cruising on the surface with their backs and spiky dorsal fin showing above the water. This also occurs when bass shoals are working over bait-fish like herring, sprat or mackerel fry. At sea, feeding bass shoals can often be pinpointed by watching for bird activity—for as the bass drive the bait-fish up, gulls and terns will gather to take advantage of an easy meal. Terns, are, in fact, the most reliable guide to the whereabouts of a feeding bass shoal, although on occasions

118

the activity of herring gulls and even big high-diving gannets has led me to some good bass fishing. A sure sign that bass are hunting is when the surface is broken by a number of heavy, splashy rises. These are invariably caused by bass rushing at bait-fish which have been herded to the top of the water.

Bass are predators by inclination; but on occasion they will accept practically any old bait the angler cares to use. I have caught bass on squid; fish-strip; whole live and dead fish; crabs, hard and soft; kipper; slipper limpet; edible clams; mussels; scallops; marine worms; sea mice; prawns; sand-eels; and a wide variety of fish fry. Even a small bass has a large mouth and, as a rule, big baits are most effective.

TACKLE

Although bass can be caught on standard boat gear, the real bass specialist usually employs much lighter tackle. For general bottom fishing from boats, for example, very light boat rods of the Abu Fladden type should be used in conjunction with a small centre-pin or multiplier reel loaded with 18- or 20-lb. b.s. line. This same outfit can also be used for light trolling from slowly moving boats. For drift fishing, float fishing, or spinning, much lighter tackle should be employed. My own choice would be a glass carp or salmon spinning rod and medium-sized fixed spool reel loaded with 12 to 14 lb. mono-filament. With tackle of this type, every sizeable bass will be able to give a good account of itself; and believe me, on the right tackle a bass is a scrapper that rates with any game fish —a real rough-and-tumble tearaway fighter which will give even the most skilful of anglers a run for his money.

Terminal tackle depends entirely on the type of fishing methods used, as described below. A landing net should be carried at all times. Gaffs should not be employed for landing bass. Where possible, each fish should be netted so that it suffers as little external damage as possible. Unwanted fish can then be unhooked with the minimum amount of handling and returned alive and unharmed to the sea. If a gaff must be used, only employ it to boat the largest fish. Smaller fish should be shaken off the hook while they are still in the water. This is easy to do by simply taking a firm hold on the hook shank and shaking it out of the fish's mouth.

BASS FISHING METHODS

Spinning

This is probably the most sporting way of taking bass. It is particularly effective in estuaries. For sheer enjoyment, a good day's spinning on a productive bass mark cannot be beaten. Practically any large spoon bait can be used, but I would advise elongated silver toby-type spoons (see Fig. 42). These are sold complete with treble hooks. Invariably,

TOBY SPOON
Fig. 42.

though, the hooks supplied are far too small. It pays to change to larger hooks, otherwise many fish will be lost due to hooks failing to engage or tearing out during the fight.

It is advisable always to carry a good range of likely spoon baits, for a spoon which works well on one day may produce very little on the next. Unless you can chop and change baits to find one which will attract fish on a day when they are being difficult, you may well find yourself in the frustrating position of being surrounded by a multitude of bass of all sizes and not being able to do a thing about it. This happened to me once while boat fishing around the Gwineas Rock. Bass were much in evidence and, judging by the constant swirls on the surface, were feeding well; yet try as I might, I could not get them to look at a bait which normally worked well. Finally, I went back into Mevagissey, picked up my other artificial-bait box and went out again to the mark. I finally got the fish to take a very large narrow spoon and finished the day by catching eighteen good fish—of which I retained three, each over 6 lb.

When I gutted my catch, I found each fish contained a number of small 'joey' mackerel, and I knew then why they had ignored my normal 3- to 3½-in. spoons in preference to the extra big lures I had brought out on my second attempt. Bass which become preoccupied with feeding on fish of a certain size seldom look at a bait which is smaller than the
120

fish they are hunting. This day was a typical example of a preoccupied-feeding pattern. The fish were harrying 6- to 8-in. mackerel, and anything smaller was ignored My big spoons evidently fell in the right class, and the bass hit them with confidence.

The following day, the situation was reversed. The mackerel shoal had dispersed. The bass were feeding on sand-eels, and only small spoons caught fish.

The drawback to the toby-type spoon is that it is fairly light for its size. Because of this, it does not fish well when the bass are feeding deep down. Under these circumstances, German sprat lures should be used. These are fish-shaped wobbling-type baits made of thick gauge heavy metal. They cast well, sink quickly and, on the right day, can be extremely deadly.

Very occasionally one comes across a day when the bass will trail along behind a normal bait, practically bumping it with their snouts but making no definite attempt to take it. This can be very frustrating for the angler, who sees bass after bass following the bait up to the boat and then sheering away at the last moment. The only way I have hooked bass under this condition is by using a very tiny spoon; and the only explanation I can give for this behaviour is the possibility that the fish were preoccupied with tiny white bait or mackerel midge and would therefore strike only at very diminutive lures.

Bass are fast, active fish. To get maximum results from spinning, the bait should be retrieved fairly rapidly. This is particularly true when the fish are shoaling close to the surface. When this occurs, the bait should work along just under the surface. A straight, steady retrieve usually produces most takes under these conditions (see Fig. 43). If the fish are

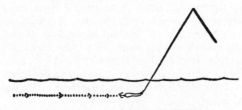

STRAIGHT RETRIEVE

Fig. 43.

121

inclined to shy away from the bait, however, a staggered retrieve should be tried. This can be achieved either by swinging the rod tip from side to side, so that the bait continually works in a zig-zag fashion (see Fig. 44), or by varying the rate of retrieve so that the bait falters every few yards before picking up speed again (see Fig. 45). This sort of fishing is best done from an anchored boat.

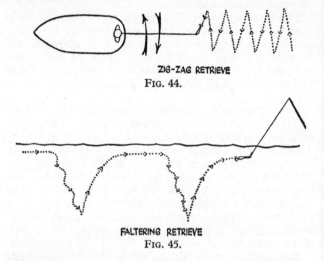

ZIG-ZAG RETRIEVE
FIG. 44.

FALTERING RETRIEVE
FIG. 45.

Plug Fishing

Plug fishing for bass is, in many respects, similar to spinning; but it is by no means widely practised in Britain. In fact, it is rare to meet a bass angler who has ever consistently tried to catch bass on plug-type baits. At one time, I experimented a great deal with plug baits while bass fishing in West Country waters and, taken on an overall basis, my catches were very encouraging indeed. During this period, my habit was to go out in a small inboard motor boat of the yacht-tender type, anchor at the mouth of a rocky inlet and fish the tide up. Only rarely did I go home without at least one reasonable bass to show for my efforts, and over a period of time I came to respect the bass-catching properties of the right kind of plug bait.

Make no mistake about this, however—plugs are legion, and most are designed to catch the angler rather than the fish.

122

I, like many other anglers, discovered this fact at considerable cost. My own experience with plugs has convinced me that very few of the many available patterns are of any use for bass fishing, and these invariably seem to be the most costly types made out of translucent plastic. I did once have a pre-war American wooden plug which was an absolute killer, but I finally lost this to an outsize bass in the white water off Point Head, Mevagissey, and I never found another wooden plug which worked as well. For everyday plug fishing, a jointed plug (Fig. 46) painted a light colour seems to work best—blue

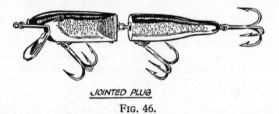

JOINTED PLUG

FIG. 46.

and silver or blue and white being the most deadly colour combinations, probably because both resemble sprats or mackerel.

Plug baits work on the diving vane principle. In other words, the faster you retrieve the bait the greater the water pressure on its valve or lip and the deeper it dives. I always find that by retrieving the bait at a moderate speed, so that it does not work too high or too low in the water, I catch plenty of good fish.

A plug which often works extremely well around or over submerged rocks is a single-jointed red plug furnished with a tail made of a number of plastic tubes lashed together (see Fig. 47). This plug was originally produced for salmon fishing and is meant to represent a freshly cooked prawn. I cannot say why bass are attracted by it, but the fact remains that

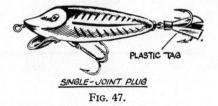

PLASTIC TAG

SINGLE-JOINT PLUG

FIG. 47.

it works exceptionally well when used in shallow water close to thick rock.

All artificial baits can be made more attractive by the addition of a strip of fresh mackerel or garfish skin attached to the bend of the hook. Fish strips can also be used on their own (see Fig. 48), but only when a weight has been added to the reel line; otherwise, they are far too light to cast any distance. The only leads to use for this sort of work are Jardine leads or fold-over leads (see Fig. 49). The Jardine lead should be bent into a half-circular shape once it is attached to the line (see Fig. 50). This will stop it flying off while in use.

Although wire traces are not necessary for bass fishing, a trace is essential for spin fishing. This is best made up of a length of nylon of equal b.s. to the reel line, and it should incorporate two swivels—a link or buckle swivel to clip on to the bait and a barrel swivel to attach the bait and trace to the reel line (see Fig. 51). The size of the swivels should be kept down to the minimum at all times, and each should be well oiled both before and after use, otherwise they will quickly seize up. The length of trace should be 12 to 18 in.

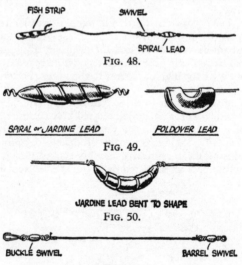

FISH STRIP   SWIVEL

SPIRAL LEAD

FIG. 48.

SPIRAL or JARDINE LEAD   FOLDOVER LEAD

FIG. 49.

JARDINE LEAD BENT TO SHAPE

FIG. 50.

BUCKLE SWIVEL   BARREL SWIVEL

FIG. 51.

124

Trolling

This is a most controversial method of fishing, which many anglers condemn on the grounds that it is practically a commercial way of taking bass. I cannot subscribe to this viewpoint, although I do admit that when bass are shoaling a trolled bait can be extremely deadly. I would go so far as to say that whenever a really huge catch of bass is reported to the angling press, nine times out of ten the fish will have fallen to baits trolled slowly behind a moving motor-type boat.

In the West Country, trolling is used a great deal—particularly round marks like the Eddystone Reef, the Gwineas Rock and the Udder Reef. West Country boatmen normally use a rubber eel of one kind or another to catch their bass. More often than not, these eels are of the type known either as the Mevagissey eel or the red gill eel—both of which were invented by Alex Ingram, a resident of Mevagissey.

The red gill eel is the latest of Mr. Ingram's special sea baits and, without doubt, the best artificial bass bait yet devised. The original Mevagissey eel was a winner, but the red gill beats it hands down. The most important point about these eels is the fact that Mr. Ingram is a practising angler who only arrives at a final bait design after years of research done at sea. I lived in Mevagissey at the time the original eel was being tested and perfected, and I can vouch for the fact that the basic design was remodelled a great many times before Mr. Ingram was finally satisfied that he could market a bait which represented value for money. In the early days of this eel, I fished in company with Mr. Ingram a good many times and, on many occasions, his eels thoroughly outfished any commercially produced baits I cared to procure.

The new red gill eel is based on the original design (see Fig. 52), but it incorporates a specially designed tail which causes the eel to work in a most lifelike manner when towed behind a slowly moving boat. Since its innovation, commercial bass catches have gone up 100 per cent in Mevagissey alone;

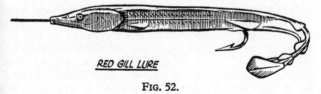

RED GILL LURE

FIG. 52.

and on my last visit to south Cornwall, I found bass specialists in Fowey who swore it would catch bass as well as, if not better than, the natural sand-eel. I know that my own bass catches off the Isle of Wight have improved since I started to use this bait for trolling, and I would advise any angler with an interest in bass fishing to include a few of these baits in his standard kit.

Like the original Mevagissey eel, the red gill has a body made of very soft rubber which has a very lifelike feel about it, the long flexible tail being moulded out of similar material. In the water, this bait will always land right side up. It is coloured to resemble a natural eel in all respects, and its attraction undoubtedly lies in the way its flexible finned tail waggles enticingly from side to side as the lure is being towed through the water. All artificial eels are, of course, designed to work on this principle, but the red gill is so beautifully constructed and so finely balanced that it is superior to anything in the artificial eel line yet devised.

Trolled baits must be fished behind a fairly substantial weight, otherwise the speed of the boat will cause them to kite up to the surface and drag along without working properly. To get the best sport out of trolling, the amount of weight used should be kept to the minimum. To try to overcome this problem of additional weight I have recently experimented with a wire line for this form of fishing. Monel metal I found useless for trolling: it was too heavy and too stiff to fish comfortably. But the new stainless steel industrial wire that has recently come on to the market has proved to be very good for trolling purposes. First, it is very supple in comparison with Monel metal, so it is much easier to control; and secondly, its very thin external diameter cuts down water resistance to the absolute minimum. I used 19-lb. b.s. wire for trolling and this had the equivalent diameter of 5.2 b.s. nylon line—a remarkable breakthrough by the manufacturers of the wire and a discovery which I have no doubt will revolutionise sea angling during future seasons.

It is never wise to attach the terminal tackle to the wire itself. For trolling purposes, I tied the eel direct to a 6-ft. length of 16-lb. b.s. nylon. This was attached to the wire by means of small stainless spiral link and single-barrel swivel (see Fig. 53). With this sort of rig, it was possible to fish with only an additional ounce of lead—sufficient to hold the bait down well beneath the surface, where the bass could be

126

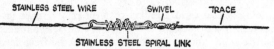

STAINLESS STEEL WIRE   SWIVEL   TRACE

STAINLESS STEEL SPIRAL LINK

FIG. 53.

expected to see and intercept it. The only lead that was streamlined enough for this was the spiral U-shaped lead already described. A roller tip ring is, of course, essential for use with a wire line, no matter how thin or supple it might be.

It is, naturally, quite possible to troll with a monofil or braided line, the only difference being that heavier weights will be required to hold the bait down beneath the surface.

There is one other sort of rubber eel which I have used to good effect for bass trolling. This is a French bait known as 'snack'. The beauty of the snack is that the weight is combined in the body of the eel (see Fig. 54). This bait can be obtained in a variety of sizes and, in my experience, is well worth using. A leaded eel of this kind lends itself readily to use with a metal line. On the first occasion I employed the weighted bait and

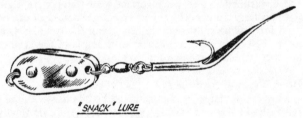

"SNACK" LURE

FIG. 54.

line together, I was fortunate enough to take a good catch of medium-sized bass, including three fish above 6 lb.—by no means monsters, but good fish and ample proof of the snack's fish-appeal when trailed behind a moving boat.

Trolling calls for continual experiment. It is never possible to predict just how far behind a boat the bass will feed on any one particular day. I have known fish to pick up a bait almost as soon as it has been lowered into the water. On other occasions, I have only had strikes when the bait has been trailing 50 or 60 yards astern of the boat. Some days, of course, the bass are shoaling thickly on or just under the surface; on others, they are feeding deep down. So the angler who decides to troll must be prepared at all times to experiment with

127

weights, rigs and distances to try to ascertain what the fish are doing at that time. Feeding patterns may change several times during a single day. When one productive combination fails, the angler must adapt his tackle until the fresh feeding level is discovered. The same applies to speed of retrieve. There are days when the bass will only show interest in a fast-moving bait. On others, when the fish are feeling sluggish, they will only strike at a bait fished behind a boat whose motors are just, and only just, ticking over.

The worst part about trolling for bass is when a huge shoal of fish are located which refuse to take the slightest interest in any bait the angler cares to use. I have experienced this situation myself: once close to the Eddystone Lighthouse, and once off the Lizard. On both occasions, I tried a variety of bait combinations and trolling speeds to no avail. Although bass could be seen on all sides of the boat, I finally left the shoal when I began to foul-hook fish—for no angler likes to snag his catch in the back or belly. This negative reaction almost always occurs in periods of prolonged hot calm weather, and I can only conclude that the bass become torpid and disinclined to feed when surface temperatures are high.

Apart from rubber eels, almost any large spoon bait can be used for trolling purposes, the best being the wobbler-type lures. The huge Efgeeco piker is an example of the type of lure best suited to trolling for bass.

Other Types of Artificial Bait

Most tackle shops are pack-jammed with baits which their respective makers invariably claim to be deadly or totally irresistible to fish. All anglers are continually searching for ways of building up their catches and, where artificial baits are concerned, few anglers can pass a new type of bait without buying one just to see how good it is. Quite honestly, the vast majority of artificial baits now on sale are rubbish. Most will catch fish on occasion, but few are better-than-average fish càtchers. Nevertheless, they sell to the angler in enormous quantities.

Over the years, practically every living thing that a bass might conceivably eat has been reproduced in plastic, foam rubber or metal. At one time I was sent a number of allegedly deadly baits to try out. Although I did give most of them a fairly exhaustive trial, very few impressed me to any great extent. Because of this, I would advise the ordinary bass
128

angler who wishes to experiment with artificial baits to stick to the patterns that are known to catch fish. Briefly, these are wobbling- or bar-type metal lures, jointed plug baits, and artificial eels of the Mevagissey or red gill type. As regards eel-type lures, always make absolutely certain that the baits you buy have flexible tails. Some patterns are made of stiff plastic. These are useless and should be avoided at all costs.

The main secret of spinning or trolling is to have complete confidence in the bait you are using. Far too many anglers carry a boxful of colourful lures and spend the whole day changing from one bait to another. This is wrong. A bait must be in the water to catch fish, and the longer it stays there the better its chance of success. So limit your bait collection as much as possible, and thus eliminate the desire to constantly try this or that bait in the hope that it will bring instant success.

BOTTOM FISHING

Strangely enough, bottom fishing from an anchored or drifting boat has never been a particularly popular method of bass fishing—probably because most successful bass men are, by nature, restless anglers who like to keep themselves or their baits continually on the move. Personally, I like to fish both ways; and having had a number of good bass while bottom fishing, I now tend to regard this style of angling as a worthwhile occupation.

In the Hurst Castle and Alum Bay areas of the Solent, I do quite a lot of bottom fishing for big bass. Although I have yet to take a double-figure bass from either of these marks, both have produced very big specimens to bottom fishermen. The largest bass I can trace from Alum Bay weighed 16 lb. and was taken on a legered live bait (see Fig. 55). The best at Hurst was a thirteen-pounder which fell to a legered squid bait. In the West Country estuaries, bottom fishing is also practised by boat anglers, particularly on the Fowey River in south Cornwall—an area which probably produces more bass per annum than anywhere in the British Isles, with the possible exception of some of the southern Irish storm beaches.

For basic bottom fishing using a whole dead fish, squid or crab bait, it is advisable to use a plain running leger with a hook trace no more than 4 ft. in length. Heavy rods, reels and lines should not be used for this work. The lighter you fish

129

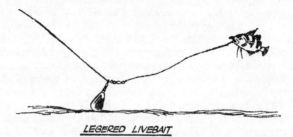

LEGERED LIVEBAIT

FIG. 55.

the more sensitive is your tackle. Despite their obvious speed and power, bass are often shy-biting fish which will pick up a bait very gently, giving only a tiny bite indication in the process. With heavy tackle, this sort of bite may well go completely undetected. The fish will either suck the bait off the hook or drop it, without the angler being aware of its presence. With light, sensitive tackle, the rod tip will give a clear indication of a bite no matter how cautiously the fish takes the bait.

While bottom fishing in this way I have caught a number of fine bass and, although I have taken fish well on squid or fish baits, 'peeler' or soft crabs have always produced the greatest amount of bites per session. Peeler or soft crabs are almost impossible to buy from bait dealers, and most anglers make a point of collecting their own supply the day before they intend to fish. Crabs change their shell once or twice a year, of course, and it is during the first part of this act—when the old shell splits down the middle—that the crab becomes a peeler. Later, when it has entirely shed its old cracked shell and is busily engaged in growing a new one, it is known as a 'softie' or 'paper-backed crab'. Naturally, during this moulting stage the crab is very vulnerable, and to avoid danger it will take refuge in any suitable retreat it can find. Once it has located a hide-out, it will remain there until its new shell has hardened sufficiently for it to be relatively safe.

During both stages, moulting crabs are much sought after as bait, and many anglers construct special traps to catch them in quantity. These traps are designed so that the moulting crab, while searching for a safe retreat, will be tempted to crawl inside and stay there until the bait collector comes round to empty them. Sections of old ceramic piping

130

make good crab traps. These should be placed among weed-covered rock, well below the high-tide line.

The angler who does not wish to use traps of this kind can usually collect a few bait crabs by turning over piles of thick weed close to projecting rocks, where moulting crabs usually collect. An hour spent poking about under the living weed clumps will usually produce a reasonable supply of bait-sized soft or peeler crabs.

Baiting up with soft and peeler crabs depends a great deal on the size of the crab itself. Small and medium ones can be used whole (see Fig. 56) with the claws removed. Or they can be used whole and alive. This is the best way, in my opinion. To use a paper-backed crab and keep it alive, the hook point and bend should be passed through the channel behind its eyes (see Fig. 57). Very large peeler crabs can be

CRAB TIED TO HOOK WITH
LARGE CLAWS REMOVED

FIG. 56.

used whole or cut in half. Naturally, without their shell these baits are very soft and it pays to tie them on to the hook with a length of soft wool.

Crabs in all stages of development can be kept alive for several days in a bucket containing a little sea water and a lot of fresh damp seaweed. Where possible, a container full of crabs should be kept in a cool, dark place.

Bass are very adept at sucking crab baits off the hook, so it is advisable to hold the rod at all times and strike at the slightest indication of a bite. Squid and fish baits are much tougher, and bass tend to take them in a different way. So when either of these two baits is used, the rod can be held or laid down according to preference.

CRAB HOOKED THROUGH
EYE SOCKETS

FIG. 57.

BOTTOM FISHING WITH LIVE FISH BAITS

Despite the fact that bass are known predators, few bass anglers bother to use live bait other than sand-eel. I have never understood why. A small live wrasse, blenny, goby or pouting makes an excellent bass bait. Live sand-eels have long been regarded as a top bass bait. In the West Country, where sand-eels are common, charter-boat skippers and anglers alike make a habit of catching a plentiful supply of these active little fish whenever a serious bass-fishing expedition is planned.

To catch sand-eels in large quantities, a properly constructed fine-meshed seine net should be employed; for gathering

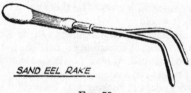

SAND EEL RAKE

FIG. 58.

a few dozen eels, a sand-eel rake (see Fig. 58) can be used. Raking sand-eels calls for practice, but once the technique is mastered it is a simple enough job to procure ample eels for a day's fishing. Sand-eels come inshore to avoid predators,

and they bury themselves in the loose sand at the sea's edge.
By pulling the rake firmly through the sand in the shallows,
the eels can be flipped out and caught in the free hand.

Keeping sand-eels alive is far more difficult than catching
them. The only practical container to use is a specially constructed courge or wooden bait-box (see Fig. 59) which has
perforated sides. Captured eels should be placed in this as
quickly as possible, and the box should be allowed to float at

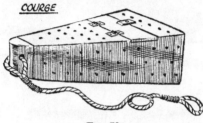

FIG. 59.

all times so that the fresh sea water continually filters through
the perforations and keeps the eels alive. Sand-eels are
extremely delicate little creatures. At the slightest trace of
rough handling or if the water becomes stale they will turn,
belly-up, and die. So take my advice and handle them as little
as possible; and always make absolutely certain that the bait-
box is well perforated and clean. Dirty bait-boxes will quickly
destroy freshly caught sand-eels.

Sand-eels can be fished on a running leger, but they work
best when allowed to swim as freely as possible. At Fowey,
where boat fishing for bass with live sand-eel baits has been
brought to a fine art, the technique of long-link legering
approaches perfection. Only very small leads are used, and
these are stopped 5 ft. from the hook. The method is to drop
the bait into the water and pay out 20 to 40 ft. of line through
the eye of the lead (see Fig. 60). Once the bait is well astern
of the boat, the lead is lowered to the bottom in the normal
way, leaving the live eel to range about naturally at the end of
a very long tether. This technique is so effective that local
bass specialists think nothing of catching a dozen or more
prime bass in a single session.

Where the tidal current is fast, live eels should be hooked
once through the lower part of the jaw (see Fig. 61). This
allows the eel to move freely and breathe easily at all times.

133

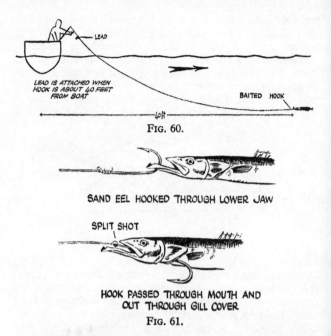

LEAD

LEAD IS ATTACHED WHEN
HOOK IS ABOUT 40 FEET
FROM BOAT

BAITED HOOK

40 ft

FIG. 60.

SAND EEL HOOKED THROUGH LOWER JAW

SPLIT SHOT

HOOK PASSED THROUGH MOUTH AND
OUT THROUGH GILL COVER

FIG. 61.

Some anglers, however, prefer to pass the hook through the eel's mouth so that the point and barb project from its gill slit. This gives a firmer hook hold but makes it difficult for the eels to breathe. I find that sand-eels hooked in this fashion usually expire very quickly. Under slack-water conditions, the eel can be mounted by passing the hook through the flesh of the back, just behind the head. This gives a good hook hold but, again, tends to kill the eel very quickly. Dead sand-eels can be used, of course, but they are far less effective than live eels where bass are concerned.

Bass generally take sand-eels very decisively. Usually, the first indication that a fish has found the bait comes when the rod tip pulls hard round. At Fowey, light tackle is generally used for this form of bass fishing and the boats are either anchored or allowed to drift with the prevailing tide. Quite apart from bass, I have had some fine big flatfish on live sand-eel baits.

Live sand-eels are best fished over a flat sand or mud bottom, where they would naturally live. Bass hunting these areas expect to find sand-eels present and will usually take the bait with confidence.

Small live fish of almost any type can be used on bottom tackle, but it is advisable to use baits which conform with the type of ground one is fishing over. Small wrasse, butterfish, blennies, etc., should always be fished over fairly rocky ground, for all these fish normally live on or close to rock and weed. If used away from their natural habitat, they may well frighten the hunting bass. In more open water, small pouting, joey mackerel and horse mackerel should be used.

Live fish baits should be fished on a 4 or 5-ft. hook trace, otherwise there is the danger of them hiding under some obstruction and snagging the terminal tackle.

The size of hooks used for livebait fishing depends entirely on the size of bait being used. Small sand-eels, for example, should be used on size 1 or 2 hooks, and larger eels on size 1-0 or 2-0. Live fish, which are much bulkier, are best fished on a size 4-0 fine-wire round-bend hook (see Fig. 62). Fish baits can be hooked either through the lips or through the root of the tail.

FINE WIRE ROUND BEND
BASS HOOK

FIG. 62.

FLOAT FISHING FOR BASS

Bass are active, fast-moving fish which tend to be attracted by a moving bait. Because of this, baits presented on float tackle can be very deadly. Float fishing is, in my opinion, definitely a shallow-water technique; for even when sliding floats are used, it is difficult to hold the bait down in any great depth of tidal water. Very large floats capable of supporting extra heavy leads could be used to keep the bait down; but bass are rather float-shy, and the drag imposed by a heavy float and large lead will usually cause them to drop the bait before a successful strike can be made. The best bass floats I have ever used are based on a balsa pencil float (see Fig. 63) given to me by Major Donovan Kelly, the well-known bass specialist. Balsa pencils can be made up in a variety of sizes to support different weights and, as a rule, I carry a minimum selection of half a dozen to suit all conditions.

BASS FLOAT

Fig. 63.

Float fishing for bass from boats is not widely practised, but it can be highly effective and is probably the best method of presenting a live bait yet devised. Choice of bait depends a great deal on the area to be fished. Bass men who fish at the mouth of Poole Harbour, for example, use live pouting more than any other bait; and in the West Country, sand-eels are the most popular live baits. Practically any small rock fish can also be used. Prawns or hermit crabs make extremely good float-fishing baits, and I have also had some good sport while using elvers—i.e. young silver eels—on float tackle.

Elvers are usually fairly easy to catch in quantity, provided that you look for them in estuaries or close to trickles of fresh water. I normally catch mine by turning over weed-covered stones at low water. Silver eels are slippery customers at the best of times, and elvers are no exception—so it takes time to develop the knack of grabbing them the moment they are seen. The technique is easily learned, calling only for a combination of sharp eyes and quick reflexes. Collecting elvers can be a fascinating occupation. The moment the little eels are exposed to the light, they quickly make off in the direction of the nearest cover. But once caught, they can be kept alive in a bait-box containing a lining of wet sand covered by a few handfuls of fresh seaweed. I catch most bass on elvers which are 6 in. or more in length.

The only practical way to hook a live elver is through the muscle at the back of the head. The moment the hook is baited, the tackle should be dropped into the water. Elvers exposed to the air have a habit of tying themselves into a knot and climbing up the hook trace—and in this position, they are adept at levering themselves off the hook and escaping. Once in the water, however, they drop these tactics, straighten out and try to escape by swimming away from the boat. Bass of all sizes are very fond of eating elvers and, if the angler has access to an area where they are plentiful, they are well worth trying as bass bait.

Prawns are another excellent bait which far too many bass anglers tend to overlook. Prawns are, unfortunately, very delicate creatures and great care should be taken to ensure that they remain alive and practically undamaged during the process of attaching them to the hook. This is best achieved by hooking the prawn just once through its second tail segment (see Fig. 64). A prawn hooked in this fashion will stay alive for a considerable time and, if a longish trace is used

PRAWN HOOKED THROUGH 2nd SEGMENT OF TAIL

FIG. 64.

between hook and lead, the prawn should be able to swim about in a natural manner.

Gathering prawns for bait can be a most interesting occupation, and there are several different methods to use. In rock gullies or harbours, these active creatures can be taken in a hand net, which should be worked round the submerged weed fringes that cling to the rock or stonework. It is among this weed that the prawns live and feed at most states of the tide. A more effective method, particularly for prawning in deep water, is the 'drop-net' technique. Most sea anglers construct their own prawn drop nets from the alloy rim of a bicycle wheel and a section of fine-meshed cotton netting. The finished drop net is furnished with metal cross-bars and is attached to a length of buoyed rope, the lower extremity of the net being weighted by a length of sheet lead. To attract prawns, a dead fish or kipper should be lashed to the cross-bars (see Fig. 65). The net can then be lowered or dropped into deepish water close to rocks or weed-covered stonework

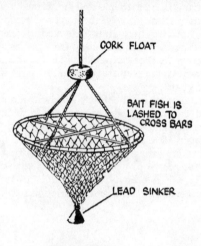

CORK FLOAT

BAIT FISH IS
LASHED TO
CROSS BARS

LEAD SINKER

PRAWN NET

FIG. 65.

where prawn colonies are thought to exist. After the net has been submerged for 5 to 10 minutes, it should be raised rapidly and smoothly to the surface so that any prawns which have been attracted by the fish bait become trapped in the bag of the net. Prawns are fast, active little creatures. At the slightest sign of a jerk on the net rope, they will quickly skip over the net rim and disappear. Because of this, it is absolutely essential to raise the net in a smooth sweep.

For boat-fishing purposes, prawns should be kept in a well-perforated tin container hung over the side of the boat. My own prawn tin is perforated on the top and sides only (see Fig. 66) so that, although fresh sea water can circulate freely while the tin is immersed, the bottom half of the tin will still retain water when it is lifted out of the sea. In this way,

PRAWN TIN

FIG. 66.

prawns can be kept alive and in good condition when the boat is being moved from one mark to another.

Dead prawns can be used to good effect on float tackle, particularly when the sea is choppy. The action of the waves will cause the float to lift, which in turn will activate the bait.

DRIFTLINING

Bass can be caught on driftline tackle—which, as its name implies, is allowed to drift away from the boat with the tide. In overspill areas, or at the mouth of a harbour where the water runs rapidly, a bait presented on a weightless or slightly leaded driftline can be killing.

Driftline tackle is extremely simple, consisting of a rod, reel, line, swivel and hook. The swivel is used simply to join the reel line to the hook trace. The hook trace should be 3 to 4 ft. long and have a breaking strain of no more than 6 lb. Where there is strong tidal movement, a lead weight can be added to the tackle above the swivel (see Fig. 67). In slack water, however, it is normally possible to fish without weights

139

of any kind. Always bear in mind, of course, that the speed of the tide will change from hour to hour and constant adjustment of weight will be necessary to ensure that the terminal tackle continues to function properly. Large, soft

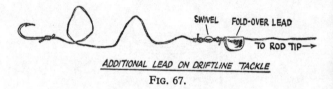

ADDITIONAL LEAD ON DRIFTLINE TACKLE

FIG. 67.

split-shot or half-moon leads of various sizes should be used as weights, for these can be added or removed as prevailing conditions change. Large baits, like a whole live fish about 6 or 7 in. long, are excellent for this sort of bass fishing.

Live baits fished on driftline tackle should be hooked through the wrist of the tail so that, although they can still swim naturally, their movements are limited, making them an easy target for a marauding bass. Sand-eels, fish and squid strips and prawns, alive or dead, can be used to good effect on a driftline.

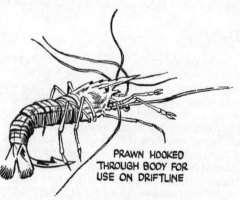

PRAWN HOOKED THROUGH BODY FOR USE ON DRIFTLINE

FIG. 68.

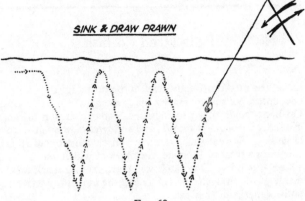

FIG. 69.

On some of the offshore sandbanks along the Kent coast I have had some very good sport with bass while using whole king ragworms on weighted driftline tackle. The art of this form of driftlining is to place the boat so that the bait can be trundled over the lip of the sandbank into deeper water, where the bass shoals wait to intercept edible objects swept off the sandbanks by the action of the tide. This is fascinating fishing. Invariably, the bass hit the bait with a terrific bang, pulling the rod hard over with the power of their strike.

Dead prawns can be used on driftline tackle for work close to rocky reefs. The prawns, which should be as large as possible, are best mounted on a large single hook so that the shank of the hook protrudes from the bait's head and the point and barb from its tail section (see Fig. 68). Prawns mounted in this fashion can be drifted out from the boat then worked back against the tide on the sink-and-draw principle (see Fig. 69). Bass can be expected at any stage, so the rod should be held at all times.

CHAPTER VIII

Pollack and Coalfish

OF all the medium-weight sea fish the boat angler is likely to encounter, pollack are among the gamest and most beautiful. On light tackle they provide superb sport; and on offshore grounds, particularly round reefs and wrecks, they grow to a large size. My best single catch of pollack consisted of 16 fish weighing a total of 11 stone, the finest of which was a grand sixteen-pounder. This catch was taken from a mark on the inside of the Eddystone Reef, one of the most productive big pollack marks in England.

Pollack are, generally, an Atlantic species and the largest specimens invariably come from western waters. Devon, Cornwall and Southern Ireland are the best places to go out from in search of really large pollack, but I have also had some fine specimens off the west coast of Scotland. I have caught many pollack off the Hampshire and Dorset coasts but have never taken one of any great size from this section of the Channel, although I strongly suspect that some real rod-benders lurk off the St. Catherine's Lighthouse area on the Isle of Wight. Certainly fish up to 8 or 9 lb. have been taken accidentally in this area, and I think it is likely that some serious pollack-fishing expeditions to the rough-ground marks along this section of the island could easily produce some remarkable catches of big pollack.

The best pollack fishing I have ever had has always come while I have been fishing marks off Fowey, in South Cornwall. Local charter boats in this area often specialise in running pollack-fishing trips, and daily catches of 30 to 40 stone of big pollack are commonplace. Favourite marks for the local boatmen are Fog Horn, Hans Deeps and, of course, the Eddystone Reef.

Pollack of good size are rarely to be found over sandy ground. The best pollack marks are invariably very rocky. Tall underwater pinnacles and large sunken reefs are ideal. The Manacles, off south Cornwall, are a typical example of a good pollark mark—huge jagged rocks which sweep up to the surface from a considerable depth of water.

I find pollack tend to move from one ground to another during various parts of the season. In the early part of the summer—say, May and June—the fish hug the rock pinnacles as closely as possible. Later, as the season progresses, they move farther out and feed over rough stony ground within easy reach of the main rocky outcrops. In the late autumn, however, the fish become real wanderers and are likely to turn up almost anywhere. A typical example of this nomadic tendency in pollack occurred some years ago when a London policeman who was shore fishing at Dungeness decided to try using a live pouting as bait. He hoped to catch cod, but in fact he caught a magnificent specimen pollack of over 17 lb. Pollack of great size are rare off the Kent coast, and fish of this calibre have never been caught there before or since; so in all likelihood, this fish was no more than a restless wanderer from West Country waters.

Big pollack are almost always to be found in deep water, whereas the smaller fish usually congregate on top of a reef or pinnacle. Because of this, it is usually best to fish at the base of any likely outcrop rather than towards the top of it.

I do not believe pollack to be true shoal fish, although they do have a habit of congregating in vast numbers over likely feeding grounds. While fishing West Country marks, I have noticed that in the late autumn and early winter months big pollack often move inshore in large numbers. I believe this shoreward migration also occurs off the Irish coast, but I have no personal experience of it. In Cornwall, the big fish come right in and are often caught by anglers float fishing or spinning from the quays and rocks. At that time of the year, the small-boat angler who cannot normally get out to the deep offshore pollack grounds will stand a good chance of catching some fine big pollack over rough ground that is within easy reach of shelter should a storm brew up.

Off the west coast of Scotland, I have had some grand pollack while fishing the inshore grounds from rowing boats during the autumn months; and I have found that in many of the deep-sea lochs the fish can be caught in quantity only a stone's throw out from the shoreline. Pollack to well over 20 lb. have been caught on rod and line, and much larger fish are known to exist on many of the better-known marks.

The coalfish is very similar to the pollack in outward appearance. Probably the easiest way of telling the two fish apart is by a comparison of the lower jaw. If it projects well beyond the upper jaw, the fish is, without question, a pollack. If it recedes or is the same length as the upper jaw, the fish is a coalfish. Tail shapes can also help to identify the catch. The tail of the pollack is only slightly forked, whereas the tail of

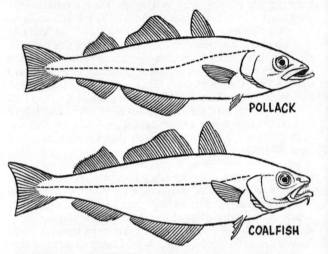

POLLACK

COALFISH

the coalfish is deeply forked. The lateral lines of the two fish also vary. That of the pollack is dark on a light background, and that of the coalfish is light on a dark background. Coloration of both species varies considerably from one locality to another. Usually, the brightest-coloured fish come from fairly shallow water. These are a burnished gold colour, with white or off-white bellies. Deep-water specimens are usually grey-ish-green, with white underparts. Coalfish are, on average, rather darker than pollack; but light-coloured specimens do occur in many areas. Pollack covered with dark flecks are also common. Cornish fishermen refer to them as 'tea-makers'.

Although big pollack or coalfish can have quite a girth, they invariably have a long rakish appearance. Both fish are active hunters, capable of sudden bursts of terrific speed. Coalfish have a wide distribution but are commonest in northern waters. They grow to a larger average size than pollack. The biggest specimen of which I have record is a 39-lb. fish caught by a Mevagissey boat on a commercially-set long line. In Scottish waters, huge shoals of coalfish up to 5 lb. in weight can often be encountered close to the shore. The larger specimens, however, seldom venture inshore of the 15- to 20-fathom line. My best catches of large coalfish have all been taken from deep offshore grounds during the late autumn and early winter months.

Coalfish can occasionally be encountered well away from rough ground and, strangely enough, they often swim at the midwater mark as well. The first time I found this out I was feathering for mackerel over very deep water when I hit a huge shoal of large 'coalies' some 12 to 15 fathoms under the boat. At the time I hit these fish, the echo-sounder was registering bottom at 30 fathoms. Stranger still was the fact that the sea bed for some miles around was as flat as a pancake, without the slightest outcrop of rock showing above the mud and sand. Later, I took other catches of coalfish from similar areas.

Pollack are usually much easier to locate than coalfish and, as a result, no techniques have been specifically devised for catching coalfish. Most of those that are taken fall to pollack-fishing methods.

Now that Scotland is fast becoming a sea-angling centre, I am certain that many huge bags of monster coalfish will be taken from Scottish waters. The seas around Scotland are teeming with coalfish, many of which grow to record breaking proportions.

POLLACK AND COALFISH TACKLE

To take pollack and coalfish successfully throughout the season it is really necessary to use at least two separate sets of tackle: a light one for off-the-bottom work, and a heavier one for presenting a bait on or just off the sea bed or for trolling. My own light outfit consists of a hollow glass 10 ft. carp rod and a small Penn multiplier. This outfit is capable of handling lines of up to 12-lb. b.s., which I consider should be the maximum strength of line for off-the-bottom work.

For trolling or fishing on or just off the bottom, I use a 7 ft. Allcock's 'Seaswell' rod in conjunction with a medium-sized multiplier reel and 18-lb. b.s. line. Quite honestly, I only use this particular set of tackle as a last resort when the light gear fails to pick up fish—for a big pollack hooked on a long carp-type rod and comparatively light line can provide all the thrills of big-game fishing at a fraction of the cost. It takes great skill to control the first wild power-dive of a good pollack with tackle of this calibre. A double-figure specimen can be relied upon to make run after run in its attempt to throw the hook.

Size 2-0 or 3-0 hooks should be used for general pollack fishing; but when extra large fish are known to be in the area, these sizes can be increased slightly to suit larger-than-average baits.

TROLLING

Trolling from a moving boat is the method most favoured by professional fishermen who catch pollack on a commercial basis for crab or lobster bait. The angler can adapt this technique quite easily for sport fishing. Trolling should be used for fishing shallow inshore reefs from a small boat powered either by oars or a well-throttled-down outboard motor. I find that when I fish from a motor-driven boat the fish tend to stay well behind the boat and can only be caught when there is a lot of line streaming out astern. From a rowed boat, however, the opposite applies and the fish will very often come to a lure trolled close behind the transom. Trolling a lure behind a boat has the advantage of showing the bait to fish scattered over a wide area.

Choice of bait depends on personal preference. Some anglers swear by a natural sand-eel bait for trolling purposes, whereas other equally experienced and successful fishermen consider a rubber eel to be the deadliest of all trolling baits. Cornish pollack-men are great believers in a good big rubber eel for pollack, and in Scotland I found that many commercial fishermen used similar baits for catching big coalfish as well. The best 'eels' are made of soft, pliable surgical rubber. Unfortunately, they are not always easy to get. Many tackle shops stock eels made out of stiff rubber or plastic, but these should be avoided. An artificial eel is only attractive to pollack and coalfish if its tail is flexible enough to waggle as the bait is towed through the water. A stiff-tailed eel rotates, and this unnatural action will normally cause hungry fish to shy away without striking at the bait. Many commercially produced eels are far too small for pollack or coalfish. In my experience, it is advisable to use eels of 8 to 10 in. in length—particularly when fishing on a mark noted for large fish. There are now some large Norwegian-made eels on the

British market which are fitted with big hooks. Although I have only used them on a few occasions, they seem ideal for both pollack and coalfish.

One of the main drawbacks to trolling with rod and line is that a lead must be used to hold the bait down below the surface. The displacement of water behind the lead, however, tends to put fish off. The only practical way of overcoming this is to set the lead far enough away from the bait for the disturbance it makes not to matter. But this, in itself, leads to a problem. If a lead is set some 12 ft. away from the bait and the angler uses, say, a 7-ft. rod, the lead will jam against the rod tip long before the fish can be brought within range of the gaff. Over the years, various quick-release devices have been brought out to offset this problem, but none of them can be relied upon to work properly on all occasions.

Personally, I use a simple valve rubber stop which folds up when wound hard up against the top rod ring and allows the lead to slide freely down the line so that the fish can be brought to the gaff. Under no circumstances should the lead be allowed to drop right down to the hook, however. If it does, it will occasionally hit the shank of the hook and knock it out of the fish's mouth. I learnt this lesson the hard way while fishing off the Eddystone Reef, and it cost me a pollack that was on or over the 20 lb. mark.

Nowadays, I use a swivel some 2 ft. from the hook which not only acts as a secondary stop for the lead but also helps to eliminate any possibility of line kink should the eel start to twist in the water. Only a small swivel should be used. Large swivels often become clogged with weed and cease to function.

The amount of lead to be used depends on the depth of water to be fished and on the time of day. Time of day is important. Pollack, more so than coalfish, tend to change their feeding level to suit the amount of light that penetrates the water. During the middle part of the day, for example, when light intensity is at its highest, the fish almost invariably stay as close to the bottom as possible. On dull days or in the late evening, when the light fades considerably, the fish will rise higher in the water and may be found at any level between midwater and the surface. I have had several pollack of over 12 lb. on lures which have been working only a couple of feet beneath the surface. These catches have all been made at twilight on calm sultry days, when light intensity has been low and sea and air temperatures have been high.

Tide speed also affects feeding levels to some extent. At the full run of an ebb or flood tide the fish often rise well off the bottom. By changing leads and adjusting the speed of the boat to suit each changing stage of the day and tide, it is possible to catch far more fish than the man who is content to troll at one level on all occasions.

I like to use a long line when trolling, particularly if I am using a powered boat. There are times when the fish will snatch avidly at a lure fished only a few yards behind the boat, but as a general rule you will catch more fish with a lure trolled 60 or more yards astern than you will with a bait towed along close behind a boat.

A Word of Warning

When fishing over shallow reefs, always make a wide arc when turning. A sharp turn will cause the line between boat and bait to fall slack, which could, and often does, allow the lure to snag up on the sea bed.

Really light tackle should not be used for this sort of work, for continual trolling soon puts a permanent set in a light rod. I much prefer to use the solid glass Seaswell rod mentioned in the tackle section.

Trolling can be an exciting method of catching both pollack and coalfish. On a good day, it will produce immense bags of large fish. From my own point of view, it is a technique I use mainly when exploring new ground because it quickly shows up the potential of a strange mark. Apart from this, I have a preference for the following method particularly for pollack fishing, for which it was originally devised.

CATCHING POLLACK ON LIVE SAND-EEL BAITS

The Cornish are great pollack fishermen and it is only natural, I suppose, that they have developed a style of angling which can be relied upon to catch large pollack on most occasions. Fowey is the pollack-fishing centre of Cornwall, mainly because local boatmen can always use a fine-meshed seine net to catch regular supplies of large lively sand-eels from the sand-bars of the Fowey Estuary.

Catching sand-eels can be almost as much fun as catching pollack. Whenever I go down to Fowey for a sea-angling holiday, I invariably get up very early in the morning to help the boatmen work the long sand-eel seines in the river. The live eels are, as explained in Chapter VII, kept in a courge. Nowadays, this is made by perforating a wooden box which has a tight-fitting lid and special fastening device. Years ago, however, sand-eel courges were made of plaited withy sticks (see Fig. 70).

Live sand-eels are a pollack bait second to none, and to fish them properly it is advisable to use light tackle at all times—the carp-type rod, small reel and light line being ideal for use with the live eel baits. To fish the eel correctly, only a

WITHY COURGE

FIG. 70.

light lead should be used. I find that a ½ or 1 oz. spiral or barrel lead (see Fig. 71) is usually sufficient to hold the bait down—particularly in West Country waters, where tides are generally fairly slack. With a 10 ft. rod, I normally use an 8- or 9-ft. trace, this being attached to the reel line by a small barrel swivel. The lead should set directly against this swivel.

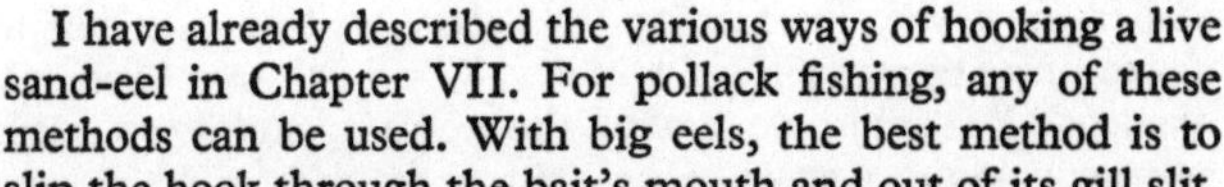

DRIFTLINE RIG FOR SANDEEL FISHING

½ oz BARREL LEAD   TRACE

FIG. 71.

I have already described the various ways of hooking a live sand-eel in Chapter VII. For pollack fishing, any of these methods can be used. With big eels, the best method is to slip the hook through the bait's mouth and out of its gill slit. The point of the hook can then be snicked through the belly-skin of the eel. This gives a firm hook-hold—which is essential, for big pollack are adept at nipping a lightly hooked bait off the hook. The size of the hook depends on the size of the bait. Large eels, for example, should be mounted on a size 3-0 or 4-0 hook.

149

Once the bait is attached, the tackle should be lowered gently into the water and allowed to run out until the lead touches the bottom. Never drop the bait heavily into the water. A sudden shock may well kill it—and a dead sand-eel is a poor fish-catcher in comparison with a live one. When the lead hits bottom, the tackle can either be left as it is or slowly reeled up. Both methods catch fish well, but when the fish are in a finicky mood the moving bait is more likely to produce results.

Large pollack are often shy biters. The first time they snap at the bait, they will barely move the rod tip. To strike at this first indication is a mistake. It pays to wait for the fish to really pull the rod tip over before making any attempt to set the hook.

The moment a good pollack is hooked, it will make a wild power-dive towards the bottom. Because of this, the drag mechanism on the reel must be set lightly so that the fish can take line, otherwise a breakage will be inevitable. Newcomers to pollack fishing usually get 'smashed' in this way a number of times before they learn to adjust their reel drag correctly. Unfortunately, the first burst of power from a hooked pollack is often its last. These fish tend to burn themselves out very quickly indeed. There is a theory that the sudden change of water pressure as the fish plunges into the depths distends its swim-bladder to such an extent that the fish is rendered incapable of continuing the fight. There is probably a lot of truth in this, for it is noticeable that large pollack hooked in shallow water usually fight longer and harder than fish of similar size taken from deep-water marks.

Once the taking depth is found, the fish will often stay at the same level for some length of time. In Cornwall, many anglers mark their line at the exact depth by means of a section of rubber band tied directly round the line. As I said earlier, however, the feeding level may well change half a dozen times or more in a single day. When fish stop biting at one level, it is advisable to work the tackle up and down until you make contact again. I love this form of fishing for big pollack and feel that, for sheer excitement, few other aspects of angling can compare with it.

In Scotland and, to a lesser extent, in Ireland I have used a similar method to catch both pollack and large coalfish. Unfortunately, I have never been able to secure live sand-eels in either country and have had to use long narrow fish-strip baits as a substitute. One of the best baits I tried in Scotland was an 8-in. strip cut from the white belly of a freshly caught flounder. This worked better than a similar strip cut from a fresh mackerel.

ON-THE-BOTTOM TACKLE

I have caught many good pollack and coalfish while fishing with bottom tackle from both an anchored and a drifting boat. Although I have caught good fish on legered baits, I much prefer to use a form of paternoster for this type of fishing. I make up the paternoster as follows: first I tie a three-way swivel directly to the end of the reel line; then I attach a 2-ft. length of 12- or 14-lb. nylon to the middle eye of the swivel; and finally, I fasten a 3 ft. length of similar line to the lower swivel eye, to the loose end of which the lead can be tied. The size of the weight depends on the speed of the tide: as a rough guide, the lead should be just heavy enough to hold bottom without rolling away. Bomb or pyramid leads (see Fig. 72) are the best shapes to use for this type of fishing.

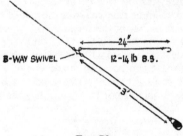

Fig. 72.

Bait can be either a live sand-eel or elongated strip of fish skin. When fishing from an anchored boat, it is advisable to bounce the bait over the sea bed by lifting and lowering the rod tip and releasing a yard or two of line at regular intervals. I have used this rig very successfully while pollack fishing on the foghorn mark off Fowey and also off the Dodman Head south of Mevagissey.

In the late summer and autumn months, when the pollack and coalfish move away from the main rock pinnacles on to flatter ground, I find that I get most fish by drifting the boat

151

with the tide. The tackle is sent down in the usual way until the lead touches bottom, then it is dragged along gently over the sea bed until a fish spots it. This sort of fishing can lead to some surprise catches; for quite apart from pollack or coalfish, a drifted paternoster will pick up haddock, cod, ling and sea bream. On one occasion which I remember only too clearly, it produced a 40-lb. monkfish which fought like a tiger on the light tackle I was using.

FLOAT FISHING

For small-boat work on shallow inshore reefs, float fishing can be quite a killing technique. Live sand-eels, elvers and prawns make the best baits for this form of angling. I am particularly fond of using large elvers as a float-fishing bait. They are hardy enough to withstand the shock of being cast a considerable distance and are highly attractive to predatory fish as well.

The 10-ft. carp rod is the ideal weapon for this form of fishing, and when long casts with light float tackle are necessary it should be used with a medium-sized fixed spool. Very often, of course, casting will be unnecessary since in most places the tackle can be dropped over the side of the boat and trotted out with the set of the tide.

I like float fishing for pollack, for I find that more often than not the float disappears with a real bang. A good float for this sort of fishing can be easily made out of a metal cigar tube to which two light wire eyes have been lashed (see Fig. 73). Bulky floats should not be used. They tend to alarm a

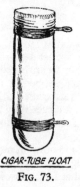

CIGAR-TUBE FLOAT

Fig. 73.

taking fish to such an extent that it will drop a bait long before the hook can be struck home. In rough water I sometimes employ a round float of the type used by freshwater pike anglers as a pilot float. These can be bought in most good tackle shops for a fraction of the price of more elaborate floats, and by the addition of a short length of plastic tubing they can be converted into a serviceable sliding float for sea work (see Fig. 74). Although their round shape gives them a

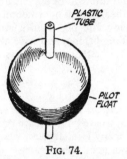

FIG. 74.

bulkier appearance than the cigar-tube float, they offer very little resistance to a biting fish and remain far more stable in rough water than a long narrow float.

DRIFTLINE FISHING

Although not widely practised, the driftline technique can be used to good effect for both pollack and coalfish. On slack tides, particularly during the late evening period, I have used it successfully over deep-water marks, but under normal circumstances it lends itself best to fishing in moderate depths.

A true driftline consists of a rod, reel, line and hook. If additional weight must be used it should be kept to the absolute minimum, otherwise it will interfere with the action of the bait in the water.

I find driftline tactics work best when used just on the edge of a tidal current of the type that often occurs just off a rocky headland. Although the driftline can be used from a drifting boat, it works best when the boat is anchored. The technique is simple: the bait is dropped over the side of the boat and allowed to drift with the flow of the tide. This is essentially a light-tackle method, and although the angler should

153

endeavour to maintain fairly close contact with the bait he should not check its natural movement in any way.

Driftlining calls for a considerable amount of skill on the part of the angler. Many specialists dispense with the multiplier or fixed-spool reel in favour of a free-running centre-pin. For driftline work, the centre-pin—which should be kept grit-free and well oiled at all times—is the most sensitive of all reels. If a good well-balanced model is used, the pull of the tide on the bait and line will be sufficient to gently turn the reel drum so that the bait runs out smoothly with the current. I have caught many fine big coalfish around the Scottish islands while driftline fishing, and have also used it to good effect for pollack in West Country waters.

JIGGING

Coalfish and, to a lesser extent, pollack fall to jig baits of all kinds. In Scotland, where both fish are prolific, these are the favourite lures of many local anglers, who use them to boat enormous catches of good fish.

There are many kinds of jigging baits available, ranging from heavy chromed lures down to light lead-headed baits equipped with nylon fibre tails (see Fig. 75). Some years ago I was given a number of lead-headed lures by an American

JIG LURE

FIG. 75.

angler I met in the Scillies. This man had used them exclusively while pollack fishing on various marks around the islands and had made some magnificent catches. Later I tried them on various Cornish marks with great success. I therefore feel that these particular lures are well worth making up, particularly for light-tackle work.

Abu of Sweden manufacture a series of chromed lures designed for jigging, one of which has recently produced a possible record cod from the famed Gantocks Mark in the Firth of Clyde. These lures make good bait for pollack or coalfish but have the drawback of being rather expensive. It is not funny to lose two or three lures costing between 15s. and £1 each during a day's fishing. Because of this, many anglers are making up improvised jig baits in an attempt to cut their costs to the minimum. So far I have records of jigs being made of old car-door handles and chromed spanners, and all have caught cod ranging from 36 to 46 lb. in weight. Similar home-made lures could also be used against pollack and coalfish. Any angler should be able to knock up a selection of jig baits for practically nothing, provided that he is fairly handy with a set of tools.

To increase the average life expectancy of the expensive commercially made lures, it pays to attach the hook to the body of the lure by means of a length of line of lesser breaking strain than the reel line (see Fig. 76). Then, if the hook snags

LENGTH
OF
MONOFILAMENT

PIRK BAIT

FIG. 76.

up on the sea bed, it should be possible to break the lure free, losing only the hook in the process.

Pollack and coalfish hit jig baits with a terrific bang, so to get the utmost sport out of this fishing it pays to use lightish tackle. Choice of tackle unfortunately depends a lot on strength of tide, but by using a wire line which cuts down water resistance to a minimum it is often possible to use 2- to 4-oz. jig lures in strong tides.

The technique of jigging is simple. First the tackle should be lowered until the lure hits bottom; several yards of line should then be wound back on to the reel until the bait is clear of the sea bed; then the rod can be lifted and lowered so that the bait rises and falls at regular intervals. Obviously, it is necessary to experiment until the fishes' feeding level is located; but once fish are found, sport can be very brisk indeed. The drawback to jigging is the problem of foul-hooked fish. Unfortunately, there seems to be no way of overcoming this trouble. When fish are shoaling thickly, one out of three caught will be snagged in the head or body.

FLY FISHING

Smallish pollack and coalfish can be caught on heavy fly tackle. At one time, specially made coalfish flies could be obtained in most tackle shops. I have not seen these lures on sale for some time, but they may well be still obtainable. If not, they are easy enough to make up at home. I make up my

STRING FLY

Fig. 77.

own from a length of teased-out white parcel string lashed to a size 2-0 hook (see Fig. 77). Fly fishing is essentially a small-boat method, but it can be great fun when the fish are well on the feed.

Mackerel feathers can also be used; but feathering, in my opinion, is not a sporting method unless one limits oneself to a cast of two or three feathers at a time. A leash of 6- or 7-lb. fish on a line can put up tremendous resistance; and if larger fish are encountered, a breakage is almost inevitable.

CHAPTER IX

Mackerel and Garfish

EVERY sea angler must be familiar with the beautifully proportioned streamlined shape of the mackerel, for vast shoals of these handsome fish can be found all round the British Isles throughout the whole of the summer season. Mackerel are true predators, feeding on the fry of herring, sprat and pilchard and on sand-eels. During the spring, they also feed on the great banks of drifting plankton; but at all other times they are fish-eaters. Mackerel grow to a weight of well over 4 lb., but a three-pounder can be regarded as a good specimen if taken on rod and line. Without doubt, on a weight-to-weight ratio, mackerel are the gamest fish any angler could wish to catch.

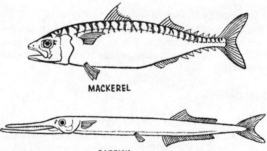

MACKEREL

GARFISH

Another hard-fighting little fish which can often be found in company with the mackerel shoals is the garfish. Anglers seeing a garfish for the first time often assume that it is some form of small swordfish, for its elongated body and bird-like bill give it the appearance of being a member of the swordfish family.

If garfish grew to a respectable size, they would probably be the most sought-after species on the British list since they are among the most active a British sea angler is likely to encounter. Once a garfish feels the hook, it's fireworks all the way. A hooked garfish puts on a spectacular display of acrobatics and spends as much time out of the water as in it. One of its favourite tricks is to stand on its tail and skitter across the surface for several yards before cartwheeling back into the sea. I once had a big gar jump clean over the bow of the dinghy from which I was fishing. On light tackle, any garfish—regardless of size—can be relied upon to put up a magnificent struggle before it is subdued.

Like mackerel, garfish have a wide distribution but are probably commonest along Britain's southern and south-western coastline. Contrary to popular belief, they make good eating. When cooked, their bones turn green. A colloquial name for this species is, in fact, 'greenbone'.

Garfish are essentially surface-feeders, but during periods of excessively bad weather they will sink to the bottom in search of food. Mackerel also do this.

A very similar fish to the true garfish is the skipper or saury pike, which is of little or no interest to the angler.

CATCHING MACKEREL AND GARFISH FOR SPORT

Personally, if I try to catch either of these fish for fun, I like to go out in a small boat which I can anchor a few hundred yards offshore. But it is just as possible to catch mackerel from larger boats, either anchored or drifting over deep water.

SPINNING

Both species are active predators, and spinning with small artificial baits is probably the most deadly way of catching them. For this sort of fishing, a light 7- or 8-ft. hollow-glass spinning rod, fixed spool reel and 6- or 8-lb. b.s. nylon line should be used. An outfit like this will give the fish a chance to show off their fighting spirit to the utmost. Neither species is fussy about lures: anything shiny which spins, wobbles or vibrates as it is being retrieved will bring instant response if fish are in the vicinity. One of my favourite spinners for this sort of work is a 1½ or 2 in. silver or blue and silver Devon minnow, but bar spoons like the Voblex or Medium Mepps are just as effective.

Mackerel are much easier to hook than garfish—for although both species tend to really hit a bait as hard as they can, the narrow, hard beak of the gar does not give much purchase to the hook points. The big mouth of the mackerel, on the other hand, gives a secure hold practically every time. Very few mackerel are lost in comparison with garfish.

Both fish seem to be attracted to fast-moving baits. It is therefore best to retrieve at speed and forget about working the bait up and down or from side to side to try to simulate wounded or sick fish.

Spinning with light tackle can be great fun and very rewarding. For the angler who wishes to catch plenty of mackerel and get some real sport out of the fishing at the same time, this is the method I would most recommend.

DRIFTLINING

When fishing alone or with one other angler from a small boat, driftlining can be used to catch mackerel and garfish. Only the lightest of tackle should be used for this method of fishing, the best bait being a sliver of skin from the belly of a fresh mackerel or garfish. This cutting should be $\frac{1}{2}$ to $\frac{3}{4}$ in. wide and 4 in. long. To work properly in the water, it should be hooked just once on a size 4 or size 6 hook (see Fig. 78).

In operation, the tackle should be dropped over the side or

HOW TO HOOK MACKEREL LASK BAIT

FIG. 78.

stern of the boat and allowed to drift away with the tide. At all times, the rod should be held; and the line must be fed smoothly off the reel spool. Expert driftline fishermen often use a small free-running centre-pin reel for this form of fishing, for the pull of the tide on the bait and line is usually sufficient to turn the reel drum so that the bait works along naturally at the same speed as the tide. A jerky bait will catch fish, but one that works smoothly is better.

Mackerel and garfish shoals can be kept on the feed by dropping an occasional handful of chopped-up fish scraps into the water.

FLOAT FISHING

When float fishing for mackerel or garfish from an anchored boat it is essential to decide at what depth the fish will be feeding. Sometimes you may be lucky and find that the shoals are harrying small fry right on the surface, but normally you will be forced to find their feeding depth by a process of elimination. The only practical way to achieve this is to gradually increase the depth of the float setting until bites are registered. In very shallow water, a fixed float can be used (see Fig. 79); but when the depth of the water exceeds the length of your rod, a small streamlined sliding float must be employed (see Fig. 80).

FIXED FLOAT

FIG. 79.

There is no need to cast when boat fishing, and the tackle should be simply lowered into the water and allowed to drift away. When the tackle has been 'trotted' out 50 or 60 yards, it should be slowly retrieved and the whole process repeated over and over again.

Never retrieve a bait at speed. Instead, work it back slowly towards the boat in the hope that a hungry fish may be
160

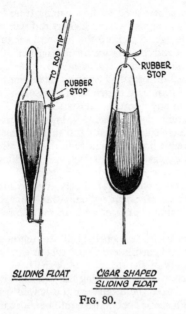

SLIDING FLOAT   CIGAR SHAPED
SLIDING FLOAT

FIG. 80.

attracted by its flash and will decide to take it. To give additional movement to the bait, the tackle should be checked at regular intervals so that the force of the current will sweep the bait up to the surface (see Fig. 81). This movement often catches fish when everything else fails.

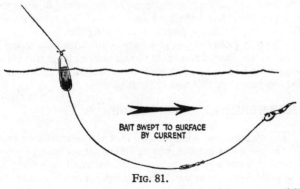

BAIT SWEPT TO SURFACE
BY CURRENT

FIG. 81.

161

A long rod is best used for float fishing from boats. When a bait is out a long way astern, a short rod will not have the necessary leverage to pick up the line and set the hook. My own choice of rod for this sort of fishing is a 10-ft. hollow-glass carp rod, which I use either with a medium-sized fixed-spool reel or a small-diameter centre-pin.

The size of float used depends, of course, entirely on conditions; but in any event, sea floats should be kept as small and as streamlined as possible. Many anglers use bulky floats without considering that a fish such as a mackerel is too small to pull a big float right under and will, in all probability, spit the bait out as soon as it feels the weight of the float. Fortunately, tackle manufacturers have now started to produce some good medium-sized floats. My favourite float for this work has a cigar shape which, although capable of supporting over half an ounce of lead, offers little resistance to a taking fish.

Some years ago, I developed a self-striking float for catching mackerel and garfish and found that at extreme ranges it hooked the bulk of the fish that took the bait. This float is only really suitable for fast-biting fish like mackerel, but it is a useful addition to the tackle-box and is well worth making up at home. The basic float body should be constructed of 1 sq. in. balsa blocks drilled out to take a thin plastic tube. Between the first and second block, a Perspex disc twice the diameter of the balsa should be fitted and glued firmly into place. The body of the float can then be shaped and rounded off, water-proofed and painted, ready for use. In action, the disc sits on the surface of the water; and the moment a fish snatches at the bait and dives, the pressure of the water against the Perspex plate drives the hook firmly home. This float is useful for long-range work against shy-biting fish.

The only practical type of weight to use with float tackle is a barrel lead. A mackerel float should only be large enough to support a $\frac{1}{2}$ oz. lead. If it needs more weight to cock it, it is far too heavy for this sort of fishing.

FEATHERING FOR MACKEREL

To my mind, catching mackerel six at a time on strings of feathers is not a sporting way of taking fish—although when I require a quantity of fresh mackerel for bait I automatically use these lures. As a charter-boat skipper, I never cease to be amazed at the way most anglers are content to haul string after string of fish into the boat. They cannot possibly hope to eat or give away the fish; and yet, knowing full well that the bulk of their catches will go to waste, they continue to fill up every container on the boat and talk in terms of hundreds of fish in a single day. Competition men are a little more sporting, and most clubs fish to a three-feather-only rule. Even then, it does not take long to catch a hundred or more good fish just to try and win a prize at the end of the day. There is no skill in catching mackerel on feathers. Once a large shoal, or splat, is located, the fish just hang themselves on the feathers until either the shoal disappears or it is time to pack up and go home.

Most anglers buy their strings of feathers, already made up, from their local tackle dealer. Shop-bought feathers are usually dyed all sorts of bright colours, but plain white hackle feathers taken from the neck of an ordinary chicken are just as deadly. Half an hour spent at home whipping a few long hackles on to tinned sea hooks will save quite a lot of money, for commercially tied feathers are not cheap.

The technique of feathering is simple. The string of feathers is tied to the reel line and a lead is tied to the length of line below the last feather (see Fig. 82). The whole lot is then lowered over the side to the depth at which the fish are

FEATHER RIG
WITH LEAD
Fig. 82.

feeding. Then, by raising and lowering the rod tip, the feathers are jigged up and down in the water until a series of 'knocks' indicates that the mackerel are hanging themselves on the hooks.

Unfortunately, many anglers are greedy and use very long strips of feathers. This is a foolish and very dangerous thing to do in the confined space of a boat. Not every feather will catch fish, and the loose hooks flying about can, and very often do, cause a nasty accident. My advice to an angler wishing to catch mackerel on the feathers would be to take a leaf out of the competition angler's book and limit his gear to three feathers only. A self-imposed limit of this kind will practically eliminate the danger of a loose hook snagging some other person in the boat.

Not only do I believe that there should be a strict limit on the number of feathers used but also a definite limit on the quantity of mackerel any one angler can catch and kill in a day's fishing. There is no possible method of enforcing a rule of this kind; but if each angler retained only the fish he could use or give away, it might well cut down the terrible and totally wasteful slaughter that takes place each summer.

The sporting angler can, of course, use a trout fly rod single feather or true mackerel fly (see Fig. 83) to catch his fish. This is an exciting form of fishing well worth a little of anyone's time, but it is only really practicable when one is fishing alone in a small boat.

MACKEREL FLY
FIG. 83.

CHAPTER X

Flounder and Flatfish

Flounder

Despite its small average size, the flounder is one of Britain's most popular sea fish. Many expert anglers have devoted their entire angling careers to the study of flounder and the methods required to catch them. Probably the greatest devotee of flounder fishing was the late J. P. Garrard (Seangler), who wrote a book entitled *Sea Angling with the Baited Spoon* (Jenkins, 1960)—a book all sea anglers would be well advised to read and digest.

Flounders can be caught at practically any time of the year but the best time to take them in consistent quantities is during the winter months. In my own area, the local sea-

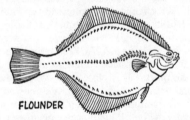

FLOUNDER

angling club begins holding flounder-fishing competitions during the latter half of December. Regular events then take place until the end of March, at which time catches begin to drop off. In fact, flounders can be regarded as real cold-weather fish which will often feed in sea temperatures so low that nothing else will stir itself to look at a bait. I have many times been out in a boat fishing the Solent estuaries and tidal creeks when the marsh grass and sedge has been white with frost and when the water which has run off the line has frozen solidly in the rod rings, and still I have caught good flounder. I have finally reached the conclusion that the colder it is the more active flounders become.

Flounders have a wide distribution and can be found all

around Britain and Ireland. They show a marked liking for fresh or brackish water, and they often gather in harbours, creeks and estuaries which have a constant flow of fresh water entering them. Given the opportunity, flounders will travel a considerable distance up rivers, and there are many records of them being caught far inland. As an experiment, my local angling club placed several live flounders in a small disused gravel pit. Nothing more was seen of these fish and it was generally assumed that they had all died. Finally, the pit in question became polluted. Among the dead fish removed were the flounder. Moreover, during the three and a half years they had lived in the pit, they had practically doubled their original weight—proof that, given the opportunity, flounder are as much at home in fresh water as they are in salt, and that the itinerant flounder angler should make a habit of fishing brackish water in preference to the open sea.

The flounder is a thick-bodied little flatfish. Its head and mouth are large and it has powerful jaws armed with sharp conical teeth. In coloration, flounder vary considerably from one locality to another. The back of the fish is usually greyish-brown, but I have had many much darker specimens. Flounder, in fact, change their colour to suit their surroundings. I have had large flounder, while boat fishing the Fowey River in South Cornwall, which have had a sprinkling of orange spots on their backs. At first sight, I mistook these fish for medium-sized plaice; but I found that as they died these spots disappeared. A close inspection showed that my fish were true flounder—and very large ones, at that. Freak flounder are very common. Although the underparts of these fish are usually white, I have seen specimens which were marked on both sides.

The average weight of rod-caught flounder is about ¾ lb., but specimens of over 4 lb. do occur. The largest flounder I have ever caught have all come while boat fishing the Fowey River.

Flounder are active hunters which feed on crustaceans, worms and small fish. They are very fond of small shore crabs and sand shrimps.

TACKLE

For bottom fishing in deep water, a light boat-fishing outfit can be used—although it will not give the fish much opportunity to show any fight. Generally speaking, few anglers bother to fish seriously for flounder in the open sea. Most serious flounder fishermen concentrate on small-boat fishing in shallow sheltered water, where it is possible to use an outfit more in keeping with the size of the average run of fish.

For all-round flounder fishing, a 7- or 8-ft. light hollow-glass spinning rod is best. This should be used in conjunction with a medium-sized fixed-spool reel loaded with 8- or 10-lb. b.s. nylon line. This outfit will do for both bottom fishing and spinning.

Long casting is often an essential part of boat fishing for flounder. To ensure that it can be achieved with the minimum of effort, the reel spool should be loaded with line to approximately an eighth of an inch of the spool lip. Where a reel with an exceptionally deep spool is used, a suitable length of old line can be wound on first and used as backing for the new line.

METHODS

Although flounder can be caught on a static leger or wander type of tackle (see page 175), the most successful and widely used method of catching them is the baited spoon technique. This was devised originally by J. P. Garrard for flounder fishing in Langstone Harbour but has become a standard technique all around British coasts. There are several different ways of using the baited spoon, each of which can be extremely deadly on the right day.

BAITED SPOON

This, without doubt, is the most deadly method yet devised for taking flounder. Naturally enough, the basic flounder spoon rig has many adaptations—none of which really improves the fish-catching properties of the original rig. Flounder spoons are now legion, but I have always found that the larger spoons make the best fish-catchers. My own choice is a 2½- to 3½ in. white plastic or silver metal spoon (see Fig. 84). As can be seen from the diagram, the hook should trail from 1½ to 2 in. behind the spoon. This distance is critical for, generally speaking, spoons fitted with longer hook-trails rarely catch fish in any quantity—although, on occasion, I

167

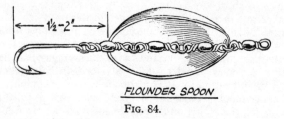

FLOUNDER SPOON

FLOUNDER SPOON

Fig. 84.

have caught both plaice and flounder on a spoon with an 18-in. trail.

While they do catch and eat small fish and other active sea creatures, flounder cannot really be regarded as a truly predatory species. Why, then, does the sight of a spoon which is obviously designed to simulate the movement of a small fish drive them to such a frenzy? Frankly, it is difficult to say. It is rare for flounder to attack an unbaited spoon, so it is only logical to assume that they actually see the baited spoon as a very small flatfish which is making off with a largish worm. The immediate reaction of the adult flounder is to give chase and pull the worm away from the smaller fish in much the same way that chickens will try to steal food from one another. This interesting theory is probably very near the truth of the matter for an unbaited lure rarely excites the interest of a feeding fish.

A spoon I have used to good effect on flounder is the Rauto Ice fishing spoon, manufactured in Sweden. The only drawback to this lure is its price, which is approximately twice that of an English-made flounder spoon. The Rauto is a very good attractor, particularly in coloured water; and in estuaries that carry lots of flood-water, this spoon is the ideal lure to employ.

TROLLING THE BAITED SPOON

The technique of trolling a baited spoon behind a slowly moving boat has long been recognised as an extremely good way of catching flounder and, to a lesser extent, large plaice. I have trolled these baits at various speeds, but I have noticed that I always catch more fish when the spoon is working slowly along just off the bottom. At all times it is essential to troll with the current, for this is the way flatfish normally swim and feed. A bait working against the tide must appear unnatural to the fish, and will probably scare them away.

168

Most baited spoon specialists fish alone from small rowing boats. Obviously, they cannot row and hold the rod at the same time. Therefore, the rod has to be laid down so that the tip projects over the stern. When a flounder or other flatfish strikes at the bait, the rod tip will give a clear indication of a bite, allowing the angler plenty of time to lay down the oars and pick up the rod. Under no circumstances should the strike be made at the first sign of a bite. Flounder like to swim along behind the spoon, gently nibbling at the bait. Once the fish is certain that there is no danger, it will take the bait and hook confidently, dragging the rod tip hard down as it moves away (see Fig. 85). Usually, the fish will hook themselves; but it pays to strike, just to make certain.

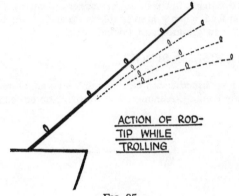

ACTION OF ROD-
TIP WHILE
TROLLING

Fig. 85.

Trolling can only be practised from a moving boat. Without doubt, however, it is the best way to catch flounder on spoon baits, for the bait can be shown to the fish over a wide area and each hot-spot can be fully covered during a single tide.

SPINNING WITH THE BAITED SPOON

Not all anglers care to spend their fishing time rowing a boat for hours on end. Fortunately, the baited spoon technique can be easily adapted for use from an anchored boat. I must be honest, though, and say that in my experience a lure fished behind a moving boat catches more than one fished

169

from an anchored boat—probably because the moving boat shows the bait to fish distributed over a much wider area and, by the law of averages, catches more fish.

When spinning from an anchored boat, it is essential to remember that the baited spoon must be cast up-current and worked back with the run of the tide in order to work correctly. Flatfish of all species rarely snatch at a bait that is working against or across the prevailing flow of water, so there is little point in casting in any direction other than up-current.

To get the best out of this type of fishing it is advisable to rove from one place to another, stopping for a dozen or more casts at each likely spot and then moving on again if bites are not forthcoming. There is no point in staying put on an unproductive mark, in the hope that sooner or later the fish will come on feed, when it is so simple to up anchor and drift on down to new ground every few minutes.

FLOAT FISHED SPOON

The float fished spoon (see Fig. 86) is an adaption of the foregoing method. Although it is a rather limited technique,

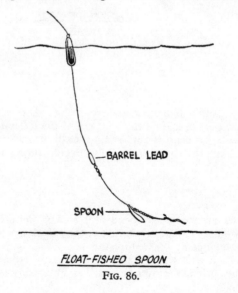

FLOAT-FISHED SPOON

FIG. 86.

it can sometimes bring a good bag of fish when other methods fail. To get the best out of this type of terminal rig, the tackle should be cast as far up-tide as possible and worked back towards the boat. Failing this, it can be allowed to drift down the current, away from the boat. The only place I have seen this method used consistently is at the mouth of the Lymington River in Hampshire, but I can see no reason why it should not fish just as well on any estuary that contains flounder.

BOTTOM FISHING

Flounder and other small flatfish can be caught on the bottom tackle described in the following section.

Plaice

The plaice is one of our best-known flatfish and, owing to its qualities as a table fish, it is much sought after by boat anglers. The eyes and colour of the plaice are on its right side and, like most 'flatties', it varies considerably in colour from one locality to another—a typical specimen being browny coloured on the eye side, with white underparts. The back is heavily spotted with large orange or red blotches.

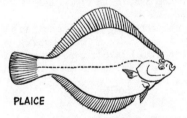

PLAICE

Plaice have been caught to over 8 lb., but the average run of fish weighs approximately 1½ to 2 lb. A plaice of over 5 lb. can be regarded as a really good catch.

Unlike flounder, plaice are basically a summer species—although I have caught good plaice in every month of the year. They have a wide distribution and are found around most of the British Isles. They are commonest in areas where the sea bed is comprised of sand, mud or shell grit.

171

Unfortunately, extensive inshore trawling has ruined many of the best plaice grounds. The result is that most of the big fish now caught on rod and line are taken from sheltered inshore marks where trawlers cannot work. Shellfish, particularly mussels, form the basic diet of the adult plaice, but marine worms, shrimps, soft crabs, small fish and starfish are also eaten.

Large plaice can be caught in many areas, but Poole Harbour, in Dorset, is probably the most famous big plaice venue in Britain. But constant over-fishing is now beginning to take its toll of the fish in this vast harbour and catches are now on the decline, although some huge fish are still caught annually from marks around Brownsea Island. Teignmouth, in south Devon, is another famed area for plaice fishing; but I think that, in time, Scottish waters will become the Mecca of the ardent plaice fishermen. Marks off the Isle of Arran and the sea lochs of the western Highlands are alive with plaice—some of them very big fish indeed. As yet, the flat-fishing potential of Scotland is practically unexploited, but with the formation of sea-angling councils, etc., it can only be a matter of time before Scotland's magnificent sea angling becomes well publicised.

There are some grand big plaice in many of the West Country estuaries—the Dart and the Fowey being two notable hotspots to make for. The last time I fished the Dart, I had a dozen good plaice of up to just under 5 lb. in weight on soft crab baits.

In Scotland, most of my plaice fishing has been done from Ullapool on Loch Broom or from Brodick on the Isle of Arran. In both areas I have enjoyed some fine plaice fishing, although the average size of the fish I have caught has been surprisingly low.

PLAICE TACKLE

Choice of tackle for plaice fishing depends entirely on the area you intend to fish. For example, the type of tackle described for flounder (see page 166) can be easily used for plaice fishing in many sheltered estuaries. Offshore marks, or grounds subjected to a considerable flow of tide, call for much heavier tackle. Even so, a standard light boat rod should suffice under most conditions. Generally, my advice would be to always fish as light as conditions allow. In this way, you will catch more fish and get more sport than you would if you used typical heavy boat gear for all aspects of plaice fishing.

My own plaice rod is an Abu Fladden—a light solid-glass rod which I use in conjunction with a small multiplying reel loaded with 16-lb. b.s. line. I find I can use this outfit in all but the strongest of tides simply because the light line offers little resistance to the pull of the water.

TERMINAL TACKLE

Plaice anglers often fish multiple-hook tackle, for when the fish are in a feeding mood it is usually possible to take them two or even three at a time. Probably the most popular all-round flatfish tackle is the three-hook paternoster trot. There are many variations on the standard tackle described in Chapter IV. Each known plaice area has its own adaptation of the original idea. At Folkestone I saw anglers catch plaice on an elaborate paternoster trot which incorporated two wire or plastic booms set one on top of the other directly above the lead (see Fig. 87). There was a two-hook trace attached to each boom. As far as I could judge from the amount of fish caught, this was a first-class technique for that particular area.

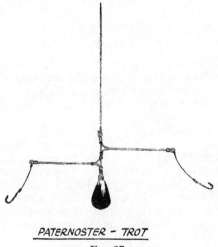

PATERNOSTER - TROT

FIG. 87.

FLOATING LEGER

A basic single- or double-hook running leger can obviously be used for plaice fishing; but in many estuary waters where plaice are common, the fishing is regularly ruined by bait-robbing shore crabs which get to the bait before the fish have a chance to find it. The only practical way of overcoming this is to use a floating leger (see Fig. 88). It is by no means the best way to catch plaice, but the cork will keep the bait up off the sea bed and out of range of the crabs. Plaice are not averse to taking a bait that is suspended in this way.

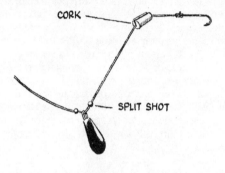

FLOATING LEGER

Fig. 88.

For this method of fishing, the line between rod tip and lead must be kept taut, otherwise the buoyancy of the cork will pull loose line through the eye of the lead until the bait rises too high in the water to attract the attention of the fish.

WANDER TACKLE

Wander tackle (see Fig. 89) is the favourite terminal tackle of the plaice specialists who fish in Poole Harbour and the Solent, but it is also perfectly adaptable for use in most areas where plaice exist. As its name implies, it is designed to roll slowly over the sea bed, searching out each yard of bottom as it goes. To work properly, it can only be used on a clear, snag-free bottom.

Wander tackle is rigged as a normal leger except that, in-

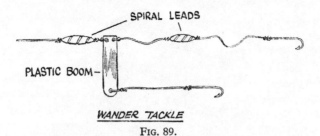

SPIRAL LEADS

PLASTIC BOOM—

<u>WANDER TACKLE</u>

FIG. 89.

stead of using a lead of, say, 8 oz. that would hold the bait in one position, a weight of only 4 oz. should be used so that the run of the tide will roll or bounce the bait slowly over the sea bed. To fish this method correctly, the rod must be held at all times so that line can be paid smoothly off the reel as the tackle rolls away from the boat. It is essential to avoid jerking the bait as this tends to frighten off the fish.

As can be seen from the diagram, the weight should be split into two equal portions so that the tackle runs out easily without becoming tangled up.

I normally use spiral leads for this tackle because I find that it is often necessary to increase or decrease the amount of lead to suit the changing flow of the tide. This can be simply achieved by unwinding the spiral leads and substituting the leads required. If a barrel lead or drilled bullet were used, a lead change would involve dismantling the entire terminal tackle. This would waste valuable fishing time; so I much prefer to use the easily changeable, although more expensive, spiral weights. Once the line has been wrapped around the spiral grooves on the lead, the weight should be bent so that it cannot slide up the line.

When bottom fishing for plaice, and other small flatfish, narrow-gape long-shanked size 1 or 2 hooks should be used.

Other Small Flatfish

Dab, sole, witch, megrim, scaldfish and topknot can all be caught on rod and line. Bottom fishing is the only successful method to use for these fish, and no special tackle or tactics are really required to catch them. Dab and sole are the commonest, but I have caught quite a number of megrim while bottom fishing in Upper Loch Broom.

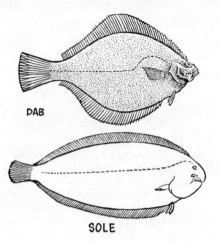

DAB

SOLE

Turbot

A turbot is the real prize catch for the average boat angler, for its comparatively large size, beautifully marked back and excellent eating qualities make it a much sought after fish. Large turbot seem to hold a strange fascination for many anglers. Each season, the lure of these large predatory flatfish brings anglers from all over the country to such places as Coverack, Dartmouth and Weymouth—for it is from marks off these ports that most of the big turbot landed each season are caught. New grounds are also beginning to make a name for themselves. The Dolphin Bank, off Christchurch, has yielded a number of good turbot during the past few seasons; and several other marks off the south-west side of the Isle of Wight have also produced plenty of good big fish during recent seasons. The Varne Bank, off Dover, has long been noted for its magnificent turbot fishing but, unfortunately, the strength of the tide in the area makes rod-and-line fishing practically impossible at most times of the year—although commercial fishermen, using long lines, take enormous catches of huge turbot from the bank almost daily.

Owing to its large average size, the turbot is difficult to confuse with other members of the flatfish tribe, with the possible exception of the brill. The eyes and colour of the turbot are on the upper or left-hand side of its body. Normally, the back of this fish is greyish brown with a thick freckling of darker spots and blotches; but coloration is variable, depending to a great extent on what sort of sea bed the fish is feeding over when caught.

Generally speaking, turbot are beautiful bright-looking fish.

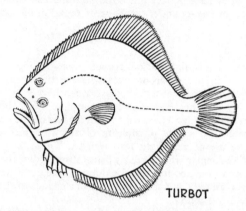

TURBOT

They are normally caught during the spring and summer months, but in very deep water they can be taken at almost any time of the year. They undoubtedly have a wide distribution but, from the rod-and-line man's point of view, they are most common in southern waters. However, they are nomadic and odd specimens turn up in the most unexpected places. A 13-lb. fish, for example, was caught at Golant, well up the Fowey River; a 27-lb. specimen was caught by a mullet angler fishing from the Lighthouse Quay at Mevagissey; and a twenty-one-pounder was recently caught by a small boat angler less than 150 yards out from the beach at Bournemouth, Hants. The last turbot I caught was hooked in less than 10 ft. of water directly out from the starting platform at the mouth of the Lymington River. As a general rule, however, the angler wishing to catch turbot in quantity must go to a known turbot ground and fish it properly before he can hope to really catch these big handsome 'flatties'.

Big turbot like to live and feed in fast, heavy water. A prime example of this is the Shambles Bank, off Weymouth— probably the most famous big turbot mark in the country.

177

Shambles fishermen regularly use 4- or 5-lb. leads to hold their bait on the bottom, and this calls for correspondingly heavy rods, reels and lines. Big baits are also essential. Turbot are true predators, with big mouths and sharp teeth that are ideally suited to catch and hold any bait-sized fish which is unfortunate enough to come within reach. They reach a weight of at least 30 lb.; but a rod-and-line fisherman who catches a twenty-pounder can be truly proud of his catch.

TACKLE

On reasonably light tackle, turbot are a sporting proposition. But in many turbot areas where extra strong tides prevail at all times, most turbot fishermen have been forced to employ very heavy gear in an attempt to offset the very large leads they have had to use to hold the bait on the bottom. Fortunately, it is now possible to obtain wire lines which allow the use of very light lead weights. These lines are a boon to the angler who regularly fishes strong tides. By using a light lead, it is possible to scale down all the other items of tackle accordingly and so giving the fish a chance to show off their sporting ability.

My own choice of turbot tackle for use with a wire line is a medium-weight boat rod, and multiplier reel to match. Line b.s. should be 30 to 35 lb., and at least 200 yards should be used so that the baited tackle can be worked well out from the stern of the boat. Remember, however, that the rod must be fitted with a roller tip ring if wire is going to be used, otherwise a severe tangle will occur the first time the tackle is reeled up from the bottom.

Anglers who, for one reason or another, do not wish to use wire lines will have to step up their tackle accordingly. A heavier rod will be necessary, and reels much smaller than a Penn Super Mariner will be impracticable. Frankly, the angler who wishes to buy a new set of tackle for turbot fishing will be well advised to purchase a wire-line outfit in the first instance.

HOOKS

Turbot have big mouths, so it pays to use a large hook and a big bait. A Mustad flat forged 6-0 or 8-0 is about the best. Make absolutely certain that the hook is really sharp before

178

use, and check its point for sharpness at regular intervals throughout the day. A large turbot, kiting about in a heavy tide, can easily tear free from a blunt hook.

TRACES

Turbot have sharp teeth, so do not make the common mistake of using a light trace. The sharp teeth and sheer bulk of a hooked fish will soon chafe through the line directly above the hook. Nylon-covered wire with a b.s. of about 30 lb. is the ideal material for a turbot trace. Like the hook, this trace should be checked at regular intervals. At the first sign of wear, it should be immediately discarded. Otherwise, it may snap at a crucial moment.

The simplest way to check nylon-covered wire for faults is to run it through the fingers. Any rough spots or cuts are easily detectable. The main problem is that once the wire inside the nylon sheath is exposed to the corrosive action of salt water it rapidly loses its strength and can often be snapped by hand. Some turbot specialists prefer to use a length of 60-lb. b.s. nylon line as a trace—the reason being that they feel that the plain nylon is more supple than the wire and therefore allows the bait to work in a more natural manner. I do not personally subscribe to this view. I feel that heavy nylon tends to become rather stiff and springy in water. Moreover, a heavy nylon trace often loses a great deal of its strength when stored on a line winder and, although to all intents and purposes it still appears to be strong, it will often break under pressure from a fighting fish.

FISHING METHODS

A plain sliding leger or a paternoster trot is the best terminal tackle to choose for turbot fishing, the leger being the better of the two. Many charter-boat men who specialise in taking out turbot-fishing parties prefer to drift their boats over the most likely ground. Others are equally sure that an anchored boat produces the best overall results. In either case, a running leger is the ideal form of terminal tackle to employ.

I like to use a long link between lead and hook so that the bait can work about with the flow of the tide. Turbot, like most fish which hunt actively, are attracted by movement and

179

are inclined to take a bait which flutters about rather than one which remains in a static position on the sea bed. There are, of course, exceptions to every rule. I have caught many turbot which have picked up big static baits intended for skate. But to catch them in any quantity, I have always found that it is the moving bait which brings the best results.

Dead sand-eels, sprats, joey mackerel and long fish fillets are the most widely used turbot baits; but if you can get them, small live pouting, dab or large sand-eels are far superior to dead baits no matter how fresh they may be. I have always been surprised at how few sea anglers ever fish with live bait. I have seen men catch and kill mackerel and pouting, then put them back on the hook without thinking that if left alive they would make a much more attractive mouthful to a hunting fish. At long last, however, there seems to be a new school of thought on sea angling. More and more anglers are beginning to experiment with live baits, with the result that some very large fish have been caught. No doubt this habit will gradually spread; and once it becomes fashionable enough for anglers to use it with confidence, I am sure that some remarkably large turbot will be caught.

In heavy tides, live bait should be hooked through the upper jaw only (see Fig. 90) so that it can swim and move as naturally as possible with the current. Bait hooked through the back or wrist of the tail will either turn broadside on to the flow of water or rapidly drown as the water floods back through its gill arches. Despite their flat bodies, turbot are active swimmers and are quite capable of chasing a bait which attracts their attention.

On lightish tackle, I have always found turbot bites easy to detect; but it pays never to strike at the first bite indication. Instead, allow a foot or more of loose line to run off the reel. This will encourage the turbot to swallow the bait quickly. Once it begins to do this it will make off, dragging the rod

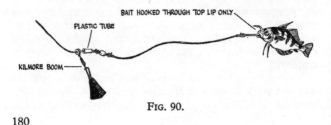

FIG. 90.

tip hard down as it goes. Then, and only then, should you attempt to set the hook. Provided that the hook point is sharp, most turbot hook themselves as they make off with the bait; and the majority of specimens caught usually have the hook well down the gullet.

Turbot can put up quite a reasonable fight when hooked on light, well-balanced tackle. Under no circumstances, however, can they be regarded as a game species, for if they are played steadily out they seldom take much line from the reel spool.

GAFF OR NET

Wherever turbot anglers congregate, a debate invariably starts as to whether a gaff or a net should be used to lift beaten fish out of the water. Both implements have points in their favour and few anglers can ever agree which is best. I believe that if a fish is to be retained the gaff should be used, mainly because it is easier to handle than a net—particularly in fast water. Many anglers are against gaffing turbot on the grounds that the gaff point ruins the flesh of the fish. I have never been in agreement with this. If a strong but small gaff hook is used, it will do little damage to the fish. Small turbot, on the other hand, should be put back alive whenever possible and to do this successfully the fish must be netted.

Brill

The brill or chicken turbot, as the commercial fishermen call it, is smaller than the turbot although very similar in outward appearance. Large brill are, in fact, often mistaken for medium-sized turbot; and in the past there has been much confusion between the two species, particularly as they frequent the same type of ground. The body of an adult brill is more oval than that of the turbot, and the upper dorsal fin extends right down over its eyes. The upper dorsal fin of a true turbot is shorter. Like the turbot, the brill varies considerably in colour from one area to another. Generally, the back of the fish is greyish brown, with a heavy freckling of dark spots and whitish patches. The underside is white— although, like most 'flatties' including turbot, specimens partially coloured on the underside are fairly common.

Brill reach a maximum weight of around 15 lb., but the average run of fish weighs somewhere between 3 and 5 lb. The largest brill I have ever caught on rod and line weighed exactly 4 oz. under 10 lb. This fish was caught on skate ground a mile off Freshwater Gate on the Isle of Wight. Brill are probably far more plentiful in English waters than most people realise. Like the turbot, they are commonest off the south and south-west coastline.

Practically every brill I have caught or seen caught has been hooked in fairly deep water, but I have had a number of large specimens while trawling in comparatively shallow areas for sole. Like their near relative the turbot, brill are active fish which live close to the sea bed, where they feed for the most part on small fish and prawns. They are also fond of a meal of marine worms. Many of the big brill caught are taken by accident on rag or lugworm baits intended for plaice.

TACKLE

Nothing very special in the way of tackle is required to catch brill, and I very much doubt that there is one angler in Britain who goes to sea deliberately to catch this fish. Most of the brill caught fall to turbot tackle and baits, and are generally hauled into the boat without being given an opportunity to fight. On light tackle, however, the brill is a sporting proposition. The few I have hooked while plaice fishing have given me some hectic moments before I have been able to pump them into netting range.

METHODS

Plain leger or paternoster trot tackle should be used for brill. These fish like a good-sized live or dead bait. If dead bait is used it should be as fresh as possible, for brill are not scavengers and seldom look at stale baits.

Halibut

Although technically flatfish, halibut are large enough and strong enough to be regarded as a game-fishing species. The largest specimen I can trace was taken on a great line. This monster weighed 625 lb. when gutted and had an overall length of 9 ft. 2 in. I doubt very much whether a halibut of of this size could ever be landed on rod and line. This was obviously an exceptionally large fish; but halibut of up to 300 lb. have been caught fairly frequently by commercial methods, and halibut of half this weight have been caught by British anglers.

At the time of writing, halibut caught on rod and line make

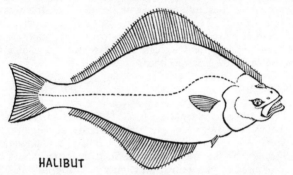

HALIBUT

front page news in the angling press—for the catching of a halibut is still a rare event and very few anglers can claim to have hooked, let alone landed one. There is every likelihood that, in time, more and more halibut will be brought ashore. But as yet, these fish are still something of a mystery— although, with the opening of new sea-angling centres in Orkney and Caithness, it can only be a matter of a few seasons before much is learned about the movements and feeding habits of these huge flatfish.

Halibut are easy to identify by their vast size. Also, the body of the halibut is more elongated than that of most flatfish and tends to be more rounded as well. The general colour of a halibut's back is greenish-brown, and the underparts are white. Its mouth is large and the jaws are studded with sharp teeth.

Halibut are a northern species, commonest in Arctic or sub-Arctic regions. No one yet knows just how common these fish are off the north coast of Scotland, but quite a few have been hooked during the past two or three seasons, mainly around the Orkneys. Occasionally, individual specimens wander farther south, and the odd specimen has been caught off the south-west coast of Ireland. At least one fish has been caught in northern Irish waters as well.

Halibut are solitary fish which live by catching cod, herrings, small skate, lobsters, crabs and practically anything sizeable they can find.

I must be fair and say that the only halibut I have had any dealings with have been fish I have seen caught by commercial methods in northern seas. I have never had the good fortune to latch on to a halibut on rod and line, so I can only write a rough description of the tackle and baits which have been used to land the fish so far caught in British waters by fair angling means. Very few anglers have ever caught more than one halibut, and we can only base our knowledge of these fish on the few specimens landed.

TACKLE

From eye-witness reports, a hooked halibut is a fast, rough-and-tumble fighter which has both strength and weight in its favour. Because of this, anyone seriously contemplating spending his time after halibut in Scottish waters would be well advised to choose his tackle very carefully indeed. My belief is that heavy skate or shark tackle would be the kind of gear to use against large halibut—a hollow or solid glass rod, large multiplier, or centre pin reel of the Allcocks, Leviathan type, holding at least 400 yards of 80-lb. b.s. braided line, either Dacron or Sea-ranger. Terminal tackle should be equally strong, and 10-0 or 12-0 hooks essential. Baits would have to be large and preferably alive.

The alternative would be to use somewhat lighter tackle and jig for the fish. At least one 100-lb.-plus halibut has been caught on this type of bait. Other fast, heavy fish suspected to be big halibut have been hooked fairly frequently on jig baits but have always managed to smash the rod, reel or line before being brought to the surface. A shoulder harness and rod butt rest of the groin-protector type should be regarded as essential items when choosing tackle specifically for halibut fishing.

As I see it, the halibut is the great new challenge to British sea anglers. It fights its weight; and so far, little or nothing is really known of its movements. In time, many of the problems surrounding this fish will be ironed out and probably many special sets of tackle and new techniques will be devised to bring about its downfall. But now we are all guessing about this form of angling and I, for one, prefer to

184

start with really heavy tackle and work back to lighter gear if necessary. I would rather take the chance of beating the first halibut I hook than stick to lighter gear and maybe lose the fish of a lifetime as the result.

CHAPTER XI

Other Fish

ALTHOUGH the preceding chapters have dealt with the main species of fish the boat angler can expect to encounter around the British Isles, there are many other fish which he will catch from time to time. Most of them are rather small, with the possible exception of the bull huss, the grey mullet and the ballan wrasse. The general lack of size of these fish does not mean they are of no importance, for many are included in the British Record (Rod-caught) Fish List. Very few of them, however, are deliberately sought after and most are taken accidentally on baits intended for other fish. This does not mean that a rockling of record size is ineligible for inclusion in the record list if it is taken, for example, on conger tackle. As things stand, at the time of writing, any fish caught by fair angling means and hooked inside its mouth can be put forward for possible inclusion in the record list provided that (a) it is above the size of the present record for the species, and (b) its capture was witnessed by two or more responsible people.

Recently, a new rule was passed by the Record Fish Committee which states that to be eligible for a British record a fish must be caught within the 12-mile limit. But few boat anglers, other than shark fishermen, are likely to go out farther than this limit anyway. This rule applies to all species, irrespective of size.

There are many fish in British waters which are not yet included in the record list. Anyone catching such a fish would be well advised to report his catch to the Record Fish Committee—and, of course, retain the body of the fish for inspection by its members. This can be done through the offices of either of Britain's national weekly angling papers, both of whom have a representative on the committee.

Grey Mullet

Although there are three British species of grey mullet—thick-lipped, thin-lipped and golden-grey—they are gener-
186

ally grouped together as all three are very similar in outward appearance.

The grey mullet is a thick-bodied silvery-grey fish with dark lines running lengthwise along its body. The tail of an adult mullet is large and well forked, and the fish has two dorsal fins—the first dorsal being armed with strong sharp

THIN-LIPPED GREY MULLET

spines. The mouth of even a big mullet is very small in comparison with its body, and the lips are very thin and soft. The average weight of rod-caught mullet is around 2 lb., although fish of up to 11 lb. have been caught. A mullet weighing more than 5 lb. can be looked upon as a true specimen and a fine catch on rod and line.

Mullet have been taken at all seasons of the year but are most common during the spring, summer and early autumn months. During cold weather they normally disappear out to sea. As yet, little or nothing is known about their winter movements.

Although mullet are fairly widely distributed, they are most common along the south and south-western coasts. Southern Ireland is famous for its mullet shoals, but these fish become very scarce in northern waters. The majority of the very big mullet caught and recorded have, in fact, mainly been taken from the Dorset, Devon and Cornish coasts. Large mullet are also common in the Channel Islands.

Mullet of all sizes show a distinct liking for fresh or brackish water and are often found in river-mouths, tidal creeks or harbours which are fed by a freshwater inlet. So far as the boat angler is concerned, mullet are inshore fish which should only be tackled from small boats. By natural inclination, they are a bottom-feeding species; but in harbours or estuaries, where household scraps find their way into the water, mullet

187

quickly learn to feed right on the surface and are particularly fond of floating bread scraps.

TACKLE

The small-boat angler wishing to try his luck at mullet fishing must be prepared to purchase a special set of tackle for the job. Heavy rods, reels and lines are out of the question —first, because grey mullet of all sizes are very shy, cautious feeders which will totally ignore a bait fished on heavy line or large hooks, and, secondly, because with heavy tackle the hook would tear out of the fish's paper-soft lips long before it could be brought within reach of the net. My advice to an angler wishing to take up mullet fishing seriously would be to purchase a light 10½- to 11-ft. freshwater trotting rod with a sweet, easy action. A rod of this type is ideal for picking up a long line on the strike and supple enough not to tear the hook out of the fish's mouth.

To match this rod, a medium-sized fixed-spool reel loaded with 3- to 4-lb. b.s. line should be obtained. An outfit like this can be used for float fishing, legering and freeline fishing. In some areas, particularly in Hampshire estuaries, mullet are taken on artificial lures.

For spinning purposes, the rod already described is far too long and whippy. A second rod specifically for spinning should be obtained. There are many suitable spinning rods now on the market, most of which are very reasonably priced. My advice would be to purchase a hollow glass rod of the type described as a trout spinner. This can then be used with the reel and line already mentioned. Do not make the widely practised mistake of buying a rod intended for pike or salmon spinning. This is far too heavy to use with a light line.

TERMINAL TACKLE

When float fishing for mullet, it is impossible to use floats designed for sea fishing. They are far too large and offer too much resistance to a biting fish. My own mullet floats are of the freshwater type known as Thames or Avon trotting floats (see Fig. 91). These are large enough to support a fair quantity of split shot and yet are streamlined enough to offer little resistance to the shy-biting mullet. Size of float depends, of course, on the prevailing tidal conditions in the area you intend

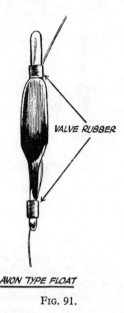

VALVE RUBBER

AVON TYPE FLOAT

FIG. 91.

to fish; but it always pays to use the smallest float that will do the job in hand. I invariably carry a selection of twelve floats ranging from small to large sizes. These I attach to the line with two sections of bicycle-valve rubber. By fixing a float in this way, I can change floats repeatedly throughout the day without having to dismantle the tackle in the process. This is a point well worth remembering. Unless a quick change can be made as the strength of the tide dictates, a good deal of valuable fishing time can be easily wasted.

To help the quick-change technique, I only use one large split shot on the line. This simply acts as a stop for a spiral of lead wire which can be wound on or off the line without trouble (see Fig. 92). The spirals I make up at home in a variety of sizes to suit each individual float. Tackle changes then take only a few seconds to complete. Lead spirals can be made by winding a suitable length of lead wire round a 1-in. nail. At one time, I always painted my spiral weights matt green in the belief that the paint made them less conspicuous. Nowadays, I seldom bother with this refinement and my catches are still as good as they ever were.

189

Fig. 92.

Grey mullet have small narrow mouths and mainly seem to prefer tiny baits. Because of this, the float fisherman should use only size 8, 10 or 12 freshwater scale hooks. For fishing floating-crust baits, a size 4 freshwater hook is best.

The only practical method of boating a hooked mullet is by way of the landing net. There are suitable freshwater-sized landing nets available and, for a capital outlay of £1, a good serviceable net can be purchased. My advice would be to buy one that has a cane handle and brass screw joint. It will last longer than the more ornate, easily bent, alloy-handled nets; and it will be far less inclined to reflect light and alarm a hooked fish than a metal-handled net.

METHODS FOR CATCHING GREY MULLET

Spinning

This technique, which originated in the estuaries of the Hampshire Avon and Dorset Stour at Christchurch some seven years ago, is now gaining popularity in many other areas where mullet shoals can be located. Why mullet will chase and take a spoon bait no one can say, for by natural instinct they are not predatory fish. In my own experience, mullet will only take a spoon which is baited, but I have heard recently that they have been caught at Christchurch on un-baited lures. I have no proof of this, and on the occasions I

190

have used unbaited spoons the fish have completely ignored the lure.

Very small bar spoons are best for mullet fishing and, although there are now special mullet spoons on the market, I find that small Abu Droppen lures or tiny Mepps spoons are the best fish-catchers I have used. The only bait that really works when used in conjunction with these spoons is a tiny section of ragworm (see Fig. 93).

PIECE OF RAGWORM ON HOOK OF SPINNER

FIG. 93.

The technique of mullet spinning is simple. The spoon is cast out in the direction of the fish and retrieved at a steady speed just beneath the surface. On calm warm days, mullet often go mad on the spoon, and to see a big fish putting up a considerable bow wave directly behind the bait can be a heart-stopping experience. I invariably find that mullet hit an artificial lure very hard indeed—so hard, in fact, that they often hook themselves in the process. This is completely foreign to their normal manner of taking a bait and one can only assume that the flash of the artificial lure annoys them to such an extent that they try to destroy it.

Float Fishing

This is the nicest method to use against mullet, and also the most effective as far as the small boat angler is concerned. I have always found that mullet feed best on a flood tide, high tide usually ending the productive feeding period. Because of this, it is advisable to start fishing on a rising tide. Depth of water does not matter much where mullet are concerned and the fish can be expected to feed whenever they can find an easy supply of food. On the Lymington River, for example, the fish tend to congregate at the mouth of a waste-pipe which leads out from a chicken-processing factory. At this spot, they are assured of a regular supply of food. Waste-pipes are always good places to fish for mullet, but in areas where there are no such pipes the fish often collect in vast shoals to feed over weed-covered rocks or worm-infested sand- and mud-banks. On the Fowey River, I have had some fine mullet catches above the village of Golant in shallow water over mud-banks.

When float fishing, the tackle should be set so that the bait just clears the bottom. My normal estuary technique is to anchor the boat across the tide and trot the tackle away from the side of the boat. In this way, it is possible to work the tackle and bait 60 yards or more away from the boat. A good tip is to check the float at the end of its run so that the bait swings up almost to the surface. Big mullet often make a dash at a bait which behaves in this abnormal manner.

Choice of bait for this sort of fishing depends on many things. If you intend to fish at the mouth of an outfall from a chicken factory, for example, then the fish can naturally be expected to show more interest in a meaty bait rather than a vegetable or cereal bait. In consequence, bits of minced meat, pork fat, bacon fat or liver make the best baits. If, on the other hand, the mullet are collected close to the outfall of a creamery or restaurant, they are more likely to fall to soft cheese-paste lures or bread in one form or another. Mullet are, in fact, very catholic in taste and over the years I have caught them on a wide variety of bait including banana, tinned meat, sausage, macaroni, rice, tinned peas and cake as well as the baits already mentioned.

Mullet bites are normally very fast, often just making the float tip dip slightly as the fish mouths at the bait. To make contact with these bites, the angler must be prepared to concentrate completely on the float and train himself to strike at the slightest unusual movement. Any man who can hook one out of three biting fish can regard himself as an extremely good mullet angler, for most anglers miss far more bites than this. Large catches of mullet are comparatively rare and half a dozen fish taken on a single tide constitute a fair catch. There are occasions when larger bags can be taken, but these are comparatively rare.

GROUNDBAITING FOR MULLET

Fortunately for the angler, mullet respond very well to groundbait. The simplest method of concentrating a shoal close to the boat is to continually throw loose samples of the hook bait into the water. I say samples of the actual hookbait because mullet shoals tend to become quickly preoccupied with one form of food. It is therefore advisable to use samples of the actual bait rather than introduce a secondary substance which might cause the fish to ignore the bait itself. 'Little and often' is the rule—for although groundbait is only intended to stimulate the interest of the shoal rather than actually feed it, a shoal of large hungry mullet can quickly clear up an irregular supply of groundbait and then move on in search of a more productive feeding ground.

My normal groundbaiting technique is to introduce a handful of bait every other cast. In this way, the interest of the shoal can be held consistently. To avoid scattering the fish, I throw in additional groundbait each time a fish is hooked. When bread-based baits are used, the choice of groundbait ingredients is much wider than when a meat bait is employed. For this reason I, like many other mullet anglers, use bread baits more than any other food. Minced bread, bran or sausage rusk can be used in conjunction with bread-paste flake or crust baits, and I find that by mixing the groundbait with a little pure pilchard oil I can make it doubly attractive to the shoaling mullet.

How you introduce groundbait to the water depends entirely on the state of the prevailing tide and the area you intend to fish. If the tide is fairly slack, the groundbait can be mixed thinly, lightly squeezed into tangerine-sized balls and dropped individually into the water directly down tide of the boat. If the tide is strong, however, then the groundbait should be mixed to a thick solid consistency and thrown over the shoulder well up-tide of the boat, so that it sinks down quickly enough to hold the fish where you want them. Few anglers realise the importance of this, but a groundbait that is loosely mixed will break up far too soon and will be swept over the heads of the browsing shoal without the fish seeing it.

In harbours or creeks where the water is slack and sheltered, the best way to attract mullet shoals to within easy casting range is to use an anchored groundbait. The most practical way to do this is to tie a length of string securely to a large section of bread-crust, fasten a stone to the loose end of the string and drop it into a place where the mullet are likely to see it. Always make certain that the string is long enough to

touch bottom with at least 2 ft. to spare, otherwise the buoyancy of the crust will lift the anchor stone and drag it off
down-tide. It is also advisable to carry two or three extra sets
of groundbait tackle. A shoal of hungry mullet will soon tear
a large crust to pieces and, unless a new crust can be intro-
duced whenever necessary, the shoal will disperse and may
prove difficult or even impossible to regroup. (The beauty of
this form of groundbaiting is that the mullet can be easily
seen tearing at the floating bread.) The float tackle should
then be set so that the hook is only 6 to 9 in. below the float
(see Fig. 94) and cast directly at the crust. With this rig, bites
often occur before the float has time to cock, so it pays to be
ready to strike the moment the tackle hits the water.

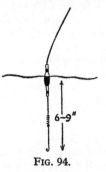

FIG. 94.

Under no circumstances should old nylon line be used to
anchor the bread-crust. This material does not rot, and water-
birds have the unfortunate habit of tangling their legs up in
it. Anyone who has had the misfortune to find a live or dead
bird wrapped up in nylon line knows just how much suffering
a loose length of nylon can cause. Worse still is the fact that
the line can kill over and over again. Because of this, old
nylon should be burned—never rolled up and thrown away.

FLOATING BREAD BAITS

In secluded areas where all kinds of floating rubbish
collects, large mullet can sometimes be induced to accept
pieces of floating breadcrust. This is an exciting method of
fishing. Every movement of the fish can be watched, from the
moment they first find the bread to the second they take it
properly into their mouths. The rod and reel described on

page 188 should be used for this technique, for the long flexible rod and light line make it easy to cast a small piece of sodden crust a long way. Crust from the side of a new uncut loaf makes the best bait. The size of the bait used depends a lot on the size of the fish expected. I normally start by using a thumbnail-size crust, then increase or decrease it as circumstances dictate.

To be successful when surface fishing for mullet, the angler must be very patient and extremely quiet. The slightest knock on the side of a boat will cause the fish to panic and disappear. I once took an angler out to try to catch mullet on surface baits and, after an hour, the fish started to circle the bait. Then suddenly my companion knocked out his pipe of the gunwale, and the fish were gone.

Crust fishing is a heart-stopping technique. The sight of two or three large mullet sucking at the bait is enough to give any man palpitations.

Timing the strike correctly can be very difficult, for the fish will often pull the bait down without actually taking it into their mouths. As a rule, I wait to see if the bait will bob up again. If it does not, I strike immediately.

For surface fishing, the line should be greased so that it lays right on top of the water. A sunken line will, of course, cushion the strike.

The shape of the crust is, in my opinion, very important— oblong crusts being better than round or square ones. Mullet have wide, small mouths and a long narrow crust is easier for them to take in one go. Crust baits should be fished on a size 6 hook (see Fig. 95).

FLOATING CRUST

FIG. 95.

Wrasse

Five or six species of wrasse are found around our coasts, but only three of them are of any interest to the boat angler. These, in order of importance, are ballan, cuckoo and corkwing wrasse. All three are rock-dwelling fish, but the ballan and corkwing are inshore species.

It is only necessary to look closely at any member of the wrasse tribe to see that they are beautifully adapted for life among rocks and heavy tides. Cuckoo wrasse are often very common on offshore grounds, particularly in the lower half of the channel, and they are easy to identify—although at one time the male and female were thought to be separate species

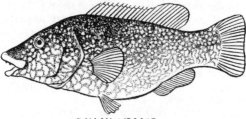

BALLAN WRASSE

owing to their differing coloration. The male fish is orange-yellow, with a dark blue patch on the head and two blue stripes running from the gill covers down almost to the root of the tail. The female is drab in comparison but is still a most attractive little fish, being pink on the back with pale underparts. There are three dark spots just under the dorsal fin. Maximum length for both fish is about 12 in.

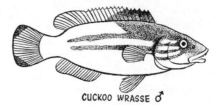

CUCKOO WRASSE ♂

A wrasse of similar maximum size but different body shape is the corkwing or gilt-head wrasse. This fish has a thick-set body, totally different from the elongated body of the cuckoo wrasse. Corkwing vary considerably in coloration, but the usual body colour is a greeny-brown. I have, however, caught quite a few corkwing wrasse which have had overtones of bright orange. The cheeks and gill covers of this species are usually veined with dark greeny-blue streaks, and there is

196

normally a dark keyhole shaped spot close to the root of the tail. The corkwing seldom strays into deep water.

The largest and most interesting member of the wrasse family is the ballan—a fish which can reach a weight of 10 lb., and in all probability could reach half as much again. The ballan wrasse has a deep, solid-looking body, a long spiky dorsal fin and neat, strong white teeth. Its coloration is extremely variable, the commonest colours being brown or greeny-brown. The belly and head of the adult fish are often netted with red or orange-red scales, each of which has a light centre spot. Occasionally, very large green specimens can be caught. These, in my experience, are fairly rare variants on the basic brown-and-red colour pattern.

The average weight of rod-caught ballan wrasse is between 1½ and 4 lb., but far larger fish do exist. My largest wrasse, for example, tipped the scale at 9¾ lb. and I have also had several other fish of over 7 lb.

All my large wrasse came before the terrible freeze-up during the winter of 1962–3. The intense cold during that period killed off wrasse in vast quantities, and it is only now —some 7 years later—that the fish are showing signs of becoming re-established in any quantity. During 1968, the old record for wrasse was removed from the record list. At present, the record is held by a 7-lb. 2-oz. fish. Prior to the 1962–3 winter, this would have been an easy record to smash; but as things stand, it may be some years before a larger fish is caught.

Unfortunately, wrasse are still regarded by many anglers as vermin and most of the fish caught are killed out of hand, with no thought for the future. This is a tragic state of affairs which, I hope, will gradually become less widespread. My advice would be to return all wrasse alive to the sea. They do no harm whatsoever and, on the right tackle, they provide excellent sport: so there can be no valid reason for killing them.

TACKLE

To get the best out of wrasse fishing, it pays to fish as light as possible from a small boat anchored fairly close to the shore. Nothing special is required, bass-strength gear being ideal for general wrasse fishing. Make no mistake, however: a big wrasse hooked on lightish tackle can be a hard-fighting fish. Do not make the mistake of fishing too light a line, otherwise you will lose more fish than you land. I am here referring mainly to the ballan wrasse, which is the largest and also the strongest member of the wrasse tribe.

METHODS

Wrasse are basically a rock-haunting species. Although they can and will feed directly from the sea bed, I find it pays to suspend the bait about 12 to 18 in. off the bottom. The best terminal tackle to use is a single-hook nylon paternoster, and I make mine up so that the bait is suspended at roughly 15 in. above the sea bed. This keeps the bait out of reach of hungry shore crabs and also allows it to waver about with the action of the tide. Even more important is the fact that it keeps the bait suspended in the thick 'soup' of broken weed, dead shellfish, crabs, etc., which wash back and forth with the tide. Wrasse are attracted to this natural groundbait, and when they find a bait suspended among all the other edible matter they take it with the utmost confidence.

Never make the mistake of using a two-hook paternoster over a mark where large ballan wrasse are known to exist, for wrasse of all sizes tend to feed in groups and more often than not you will hook two fish at once. If this happens on light tackle, a breakage is almost certain to occur—for despite their unfounded reputations for being poor fighters, big wrasse are powerful fish and their first power-dive for freedom can be difficult to check. Two large fish going in different directions would be practically impossible to stop. So take my advice and use only one hook: and when you have brought the fish safely to the net, unhook it carefully and return it alive to the water to give sport on future occasions.

BAITS

Wrasse live mainly on crustaceans, molluscs and marine worms, the best baits being limpets, prawns, worms and crabs. Hard-backed crabs the size of a tenpenny piece (the 'old' 2s.) are ideal. I catch far more wrasse on live crabs than on dead ones, and the method I employ to attach them to the hook is as follows: first the crab is turned over on its back, then the hook point is pushed firmly through the triangle at the base of its shell (see Fig. 96), making sure that the point and barb
198

of the hook protrude through the crab's back. Hard-backed crabs hooked in this fashion will remain alive and attractive for long periods of time. The great advantage of using hard-backed crabs is that they are easy to collect in quantity. Half an hour spent turning over rocks at low tide should yield more than enough bait-sized crabs for a whole day's fishing.

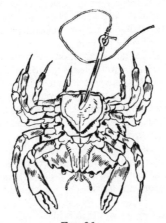

FIG. 96.

Contrary to popular belief, big wrasse will also eat live fish. I have had several good specimens while live-baiting with 4- to 6-in. rock fish, and have also had some fair wrasse on live sand-eel baits. Well-known Golant boatman John Affleck often catches good-sized fish on sand-eels. On the last occasion we wrasse fished together, he had a beautiful 6½-lb. specimen on a live eel while fishing a 10-fathom mark off the Dodman Head. Wrasse do not respond at all well to fish strip baits, as a rule—the exception being the cuckoo wrasse, which seems to prefer a strip of squid or fish to all other baits. The reason for this, I am sure, is because the cuckoo wrasse are an offshore species and are not accustomed to seeing small crabs, prawns or worms in any quantity.

A very good wrasse bait is a large earthworm. Earthworms catch fish as well as marine worms and make excellent stand-by baits.

Wrasse have large mouths, so baits should be fished on size 1 or 2 hooks (freshwater scale).

Silver Eels

Anglers who do a lot of boat fishing in estuaries or large harbours often encounter silver eels. Although, on average, these tend to be small at certain times of the year, when the eels from inland waters make their breeding migration it is possible to catch some fine specimens as they pass through on their way out to the open sea. These migration runs usually occur in the late spring or autumn, the autumn being the best time to fish specifically for eels.

A silver eel is, in fact, a common river eel which has spent most of its life in freshwater lakes, ponds or rivers. When the urge to breed strikes, however, these eels forsake their freshwater homes and make their way down to the sea via any suitable waterway they can find. At Mevagissey Harbour, for example, the only freshwater inlet is a large pipe which runs under the centre of the town. A small stream feeds this pipe, and it provides eels from inland areas with an ideal escape route to the sea. During the autumn migration, hundreds of good-sized eels come down this pipe each day—and at this time of the year, the silver eel fishing can be very good indeed.

I discovered this by accident, while conger fishing from the harbour walls. Time and again my big baits were taken, mangled and dropped without once giving me the opportunity to set the hook. Finally, in desperation, I let a taking fish run out over 30 yards of line before I attempted to strike. The result was a fine 4-lb. silver eel hooked cleanly through the lower jaw. Bait, in this case, was a whole pilchard on a size 7-0 hook and wire trace. I took five more large silvers that night on my heavy tackle; and the next evening, while boat fishing inside the outer breakwater, I got an even dozen all weighing between $2\frac{1}{2}$ and $4\frac{1}{2}$ lb. On this occasion, I used light tackle and small baits; and I found that each fish I hooked put up a splendid fight before I could lift it into the boat. Since this period, I have fished for silver eels in many estuaries and harbours all over the country and have had some very good catches.

Silver eels make excellent eating, and for this reason they are very popular.

TACKLE

Nothing very elaborate is required to catch silver eels, and to get the best out of them it is advisable to fish as light as possible. Bass-strength tackle is ideal and, as the eels feed mainly on the bottom, a running leger rig should be used. Some anglers I know use a plain nylon trace while silver eel fishing, but I much prefer to use plain braided wire with a b.s. of about 10 lb. I use wire because I know from past experience that the sharp little teeth of a big eel can easily chafe through an ordinary trace. As the average size of migratory eels is rather high, I do not like to take the chance of losing an exceptionally good fish, should I have the good fortune to hook one.

I do not, however, believe in using an extra-long length of wire trace for silver eels. I find that the stiffness of a long wire trace will sometimes cause them to drop the bait. Because of this, I make my eel traces up in two sections. First comes a 2-ft. section of nylon of similar b.s. to the wire, on each end of which I tie a link swivel. Next, I attach an 8-in. length of

WIRE TRACE

|←——————— 8" ———————→|

FIG. 97.

wire to one of these swivels, to the end of which I fasten the hook (see Fig. 97). A suitably sized sliding lead is then run directly on to the reel line, and the loose trace swivel is used to join the trace and the reel line together. The swivel also acts as a stop for the running lead. Hooks should range from size 1 up to size 2-0, depending on the size and type of bait being used.

Silver eels are confirmed meat-eaters and will pick up any fresh meat bait they can find. Worms of both the marine and earthworm type make good eel baits, but most anglers prefer to use cuttings taken from the back, sides or belly of a fresh fish. Mackerel or herring are the most widely used fish baits, but eels are not fussy. Provided that it is fresh, almost any dead fish can be turned into bait. At one time or another, I have known eels to take a wide variety of baits, including raw rabbit meat, white bacon fat and liver.

Although scavengers, eels are cautious feeders and will eject any bait which arouses their suspicion. Because of this, the rod should be held at all times, so that loose line can be paid out the moment an eel picks up the bait. This is important, for all silver eels have a habit of picking up a bait and running off with it without making any definite attempt to swallow it. If they feel any drag during this initial run, they simply drop the bait and vacate the area. If they can run out line, however, they will soon stop and begin to swallow the bait properly. To make absolutely certain of hooking the eel on the strike, it is advisable to wait patiently for it to run off a second time before attempting to set the hook.

Horse Mackerel or Scad

During the summer months, horse mackerel are extremely common in many areas, but most sea anglers seem to have mixed feelings about catching them. Many regard them as useless fish. Personally, I keep a more open mind about poor old scad for, if nothing else, they make good conger, skate or tope bait. In Britain, scad are regarded as being totally uneatable; but on a recent trip to Madeira and the Azores, I found that the locals preferred them to other species. When I tried them, I found they were delicious.

To the untrained eye, the scad does bear a superficial resemblance to the true mackerel; but the huge eye of the scad and the sharp bony ridge on its side make it an easy enough fish to identify. Although not as game as the true mackerel, a large scad hooked on light tackle can give a good account of itself, particularly when hooked in deepish water. Scad can be caught on all the methods used for mackerel, and I have had them on leger and paternoster tackle as well. Feathers or jig baits can also be used to take these fish.

Fish cuttings, worms and sand-eels make the best natural baits for scad.

Hake

There was a time when hake were very common, but intensive trawling has reduced their numbers to such an extent that it is rare to hook one while boat fishing, even off Lands End, on the Lizard, where small shoals still exist. The only rod-caught hake of which I have heard have been taken
202

by accident, and I know of no angler who deliberately sets out to catch one of these fish.

Hake are basically a deep water species and are most common during the winter months.

In coloration, the hake is a silvery grey and the inside of its mouth is black.

Hake are sometimes confused with ling for, at first sight, both fish have a similar outward appearance. A close examination will, however, quickly show that the resemblance is only superficial. The ling, for example, has a prominent chin barbule which is absent in the true hake. And the first dorsal fin of the hake is much more triangular than that of the ling.

Hake reach a weight of 16 to 20 lb., but most of the rod-caught specimens are much smaller.

Gurnards

Although there are six British and Irish gurnards, only three are commonly caught by boat anglers. These are the grey, red and tub gurnard. All three are curious fish, their heads being large and square and their bodies narrow and sharply tapered. They have two dorsal fins, the first one being

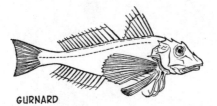

GURNARD

very spiny. The ventral fins are large in comparison with the overall size of the fish, and there are six leg-like feelers projecting from the throat. These 'legs' are used to locate food.

The grey gurnard, as its name implies, is a dull coloured fish; but the red and tub gurnards are almost tropical in coloration, both being bright red. The tub gurnard is easy to distinguish, however, for it has vivid blue margins on its pectoral fins. Tub gurnard reach a weight of at least 10 lb.

Gurnards have a wide distribution. I have caught many specimens from Scottish sea lochs and also from Irish waters.

Fish-strip baits presented on leger or paternoster gear should be used to catch them.

Great care must be taken when handling these spiky fish for, although their numerous spines are not in fact poisonous, they can inflict painful cuts and scratches.

John Dory

No angler could confuse a John Dory with any other species. Its deep flat body and huge ugly face make it a most distinctive fish. Like the gurnards, the dory has a spiky dorsal fin and should be handled with care. John Dory are a summer species which are normally caught only by accident. I have had several while using float-fished live-baits for bass.

JOHN DORY

Despite their ugly appearance, Dory make excellent eating. I have never met any boat angler who has set out deliberately to catch them—although, in the Channel, they are fairly often taken on baits intended for other fish.

Rocklings

Although there are three common types of rockling—the three- four- and five-bearded rockling—only the three-bearded is of any real interest to the boat angler. This is the largest of the family, reaching a maximum size of about 20 in. and a weight of 2 to 3 lb.

Large rockling are often mistaken for small ling, but the multiple chin barbules of the true rockling make them easy to identify.

Rockling can be caught on fish or worm baits, and they are usually commonest over rough ground.

ALLIS SHAD

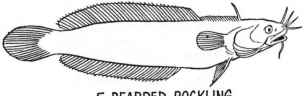

5-BEARDED ROCKLING

Shad

There are two British shad, both of which grow to a good size. The commonest of the two is the twaite shad, which grows to a maximum size of about 3 lb. The allis shad reaches a weight of at least 6 lb.

Shad are closely related to the herring family but, unlike the true herring, they run up into fresh water to spawn. At one time, many large rivers had an annual shad run. Nowadays, however, increased industrial and domestic pollution has spoiled most of their old haunts. The only river known to me which still attracts breeding shad is the Severn. Every so often, there is a big run of shad into the Solent, and occasional fish are taken from this area by boat anglers using artificial lures or mackerel flies as bait.

Weevers

Each year, a number of anglers are taken to hospital after catching and handling weever fish. Strangely enough, few anglers realise just how dangerous these fish can be. Of the two British varieties, the lesser weever is the most poisonous; but the greater weever can be an ugly customer to deal with if picked up by inexperienced hands. Both fish have a poison sac situated directly underneath the first spine of the dorsal fin. This spine is hollow. When a weever is picked up and held firmly, the sharp spine penetrates the angler's skin. At the same time, the pressure on the spine pushes the poison sac down and a jet of poison flows up through the spine into the angler's bloodstream. In extreme cases, this venom has caused death; but normally, it just gives the victim a few very unpleasant days of pain. There is a similar poison sac and spine situated on the fish's gill covers. In my opinion, the only way to deal with a weever is to cut the trace above the hook and let the fish go.

Both weevers are very similar in outward appearance, having mottled drab brown bodies and pug-nosed faces. The lesser weever seldom reaches a length of more than 7 in., but the greater weever can measure at least 16 in.

Most of the weevers I have caught have been taken on worm baits, but they will also take fish strips and shellfish baits.

LESSER WEEVER

Dogfish

Few boat anglers enjoy catching dogfish. Apart from being good make-weight for competition fishermen, they are regarded as vermin by the vast majority of sea anglers.

The largest of the two common dogfish is the bull huss—a big, greedy fish which can easily exceed a weight of 20 lb. Bull huss are reddish-brown in colour, with large dark blotches. They are commonest on rough ground, often frequenting good conger marks, and can be caught during the

BULL HUSS

day. But in my experience, they feed best after dark. I have caught many very large specimens while on various conger marks in the Channel and also while fishing off the north coast of Cornwall.

The lesser spotted dogfish, which seldom attains any great size, lives mainly on sandy ground and makes a great nuisance of itself by taking baits intended for better fish. In general colour, it is very similar to the bull huss, except that instead of being covered in large blotches its spots are small and very neat.

Both fish have the unpleasant habit of wrapping themselves round an unwary hand and then slowly unwinding—the sandpaper-like texture of their rough skins causing nasty abrasions. It is therefore advisable to take care when handling them.

CHAPTER XII

Buying and Using a Boat

TAKEN on a seasonal basis, the average boat angler is forced to pay out quite a lot of money for boat-hire charges. To some extent the overall cost can be lowered by joining a go-ahead sea-fishing club which books regular trips at slightly reduced rates. But even then, a single trip may cost a minimum of 30s. Because of this expense, many sea anglers and clubs are interested in purchasing their own craft which, over a period of time, can be reasonably expected to pay for itself, providing innumerable outings at little or no cost above the initial outlay of capital involved. Purchasing, maintaining and operating such a boat can, however, present a great many problems which the novice boatman will be unable to forsee at the time of purchase. Some of the problems that have to be overcome when boat ownership is being considered are therefore discussed below.

Type of Boat to Choose

Choice of boat depends largely on the area to be fished. Not all boats are alike in basic design, and many areas call for a boat with specialised characteristics. My advice on this point would be to decide upon the locality in which the boat is to be kept, then talk to every local fisherman, boatowner or shipwright regarding the design best suited to the area you wish to fish. This is important. To use a boat that is not built for local conditions may well result in a serious accident at sea—an accident which might well prove fatal.

Size of boat depends on many things; but in my opinion, the novice boatman with little or no knowledge of the ways of the sea would be well advised to start his training in small craft. Small-boat handling will quickly show how strong the force of the waves and tides can be; and once the technique of small-boat handling is learned, a larger craft can be purchased.

Unfortunately, many people who have little or no idea of

seamanship are buying and using boats which they simply cannot handle. Practically anyone can steer a boat and hold a course in a calm sea; but when a wind springs up and the surface waves begin to pile up, boat handling calls for considerable skill. This is why I think it best to learn boat handling in a small boat in inshore waters, where safety is within easy reach should an accident or rough weather occur. Small boats also have the advantage of being cheaper to buy and maintain than larger craft.

New or Second-hand

It always pays to buy a new boat, particularly if you have little knowledge of boat-building. There are a great many well-painted, smart-looking old boats which are full of rot, and a 'soft' boat of this type can be a liability and often a danger to its owner. Fairly new glass-fibre boats are usually reasonably sound investments; but wooden boats should be very carefully examined, particularly when they are well painted and highly attractive to look at—for paint is used a great deal as a cover-up for serious defects.

Whenever I look at an oldish boat, I normally start by lifting the bottom boards and inspecting both the inside and the outside of the hull for rot, cracked ribs, patches and filled splits. A penknife should be used to probe for signs of soft wood. Beach boats which have lain on wet ground for any length of time often rot round the bilge planks, whereas boats which have been left on their moorings tend to become soft round the stem, particularly in the vicinity of the waterline. By jabbing the penknife blade through the paint covering, it is fairly easy to ascertain if the timber underneath is sound or soft.

In the case of a large boat costing a considerable amount of money, it is highly advisable to call in a professional surveyor. The services of such a man can save you a lot of money in the long run, and the professional charge for examining the boat is an investment that is well worth considering.

Wooden boats require considerable and continual maintenance—a point worth bearing in mind when choosing a boat. A glass-fibre boat, on the other hand, will not rot, warp or soak up water; and as most glass hulls are colour impregnated during construction, it will not require painting either. Glass fibre is, in fact, the most satisfactory boat-building material available and, although by no means cheap to buy, a glass-fibre boat is a good investment for the man with limited capital and little time to spend on maintenance. On a weight-for-weight basis, glass fibre is stronger than wood. A good glass-fibre boat with built-in buoyancy is generally superior to a wooden boat of similar specifications. Glass, as I have already said, is immune to rot and its smooth hard shell tends to repel rather than encourage marine animals and growths. Glass-fibre hulls are moulded in a single section with no joints or seams and are easy to scrape clean. If a hole is accidentally knocked in the hull, however, it can be easily and quickly repaired. Because of its many obvious advantages, a second-hand glass-fibre boat tends to hold its price well.

Resin-bonded marine plywood boats are still very popular, although I am inclined to think that more and more people are turning to glass fibre. Marine plywood is constructed by laminating sheets of ply on a cross-grained basis so that there is little chance of the finished product splitting under stress. The resin glues used in the construction are impervious to water or temperature change, and the wood is proof against delamination. Plywood boats tend to be fairly light, and many dinghies are now built of this material.

Many boat-building firms supply construction kits for dinghies and other small craft, and the home-handyman can halve the cost of his boat by purchasing just such a kit and assembling it himself.

Motors

For small- and medium-sized boats a very comprehensive range of outboard motors is available at a corresponding range of prices. For small-boat work, outboards are ideal.

Buying an outboard motor can be a complicated and difficult problem, for the wide selection presents a bewildering array to the novice boatman. The overall length of the shaft is the most important factor to consider. A short shaft will reduce driving power due to the screw being muffled by the keel or transom of the boat. An extra-long shaft, on the other hand, will overweight the boat and increase water friction. Bear these two points in mind when purchasing an outboard;

210

and if possible, consult a knowledgeable boatman who knows your boat.

Inboard engines tend, on average, to be a little more reliable than outboards, but in both cases it is essential to maintain the engine. Overhauled regularly and checked frequently, an engine will give good, reliable service for a number of years. A poorly maintained engine can be a liability and a danger.

Boat Sense

I live close to the Solent—one of the most populated boating areas in Great Britain. Each weekend, amateur sailors and novice fishermen in my area take to the sea by the hundred, if not the thousand. And practically every time, there is trouble for one boat or more through lack of proper equipment or ignorance of prevailing tidal conditions and up-to-date weather forecasts. It just is not possible to take such chances with the sea and get away with it on all occasions. Although fatalities in my area are fortunately rare, far too many stupid boating accidents occur—and boat fishermen are as much to blame for this as yachtsmen and pleasure boatmen. Very few seasons go by in Britain without fatalities among boat fishermen; but despite these tragedies, most people still seem to adopt the attitude that it could not happen to them. Fortified by this stupid outlook, they continue to take chances with the sea. But make no mistake: tragedies occur easily enough with a large boat, so it pays to take as few risks as possible when fishing from small craft.

One of the main downfalls of some small-boat fishermen is that far pastures always look greener. Instead of being satisfied with fishing close to safety, a small minority of anglers will insist on trying to get out to the offshore marks where they are convinced that the fishing is better. They may well be right: but a really big skate, tope or conger eel hooked from a small boat can suddenly turn a pleasant day's fishing into a veritable nightmare. A typical example occurred in the Solent in recent years when two men went out in a small boat to catch conger. In due course, a good fish was hooked. In the attempts to gaff and control it, the boat capsized and one man was drowned. As is usual, neither man was equipped with a life-jacket.

Bear in mind, then, that offshore marks should be left to

211

the bigger boats skippered by experienced boatmen. Small boats should be confined to inshore marks, and their occupants should be wearing a Board of Trade approved lifejacket at all times.

Buy a boat, by all means—but use it carefully, and learn to respect the power of the sea. Professional fishermen take no chances with it, and amateurs should be even more cautious.

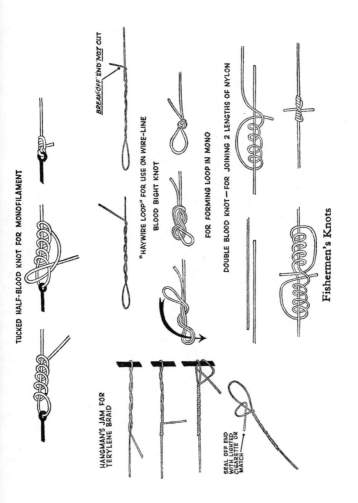

TUCKED HALF-BLOOD KNOT FOR MONOFILAMENT

BREAK-OFF END *NOT* CUT

"HAYWIRE LOOP" FOR USE ON WIRE-LINE

BLOOD BIGHT KNOT

FOR FORMING LOOP IN MONO

DOUBLE BLOOD KNOT—FOR JOINING 2 LENGTHS OF NYLON

HANGMAN'S JAM FOR
TERYLENE BRAID

SEAL OFF END
WITH LIGHTED
CIGARETTE OR
MATCH TIE

Fishermen's Knots

Index